VOM Books

The publishing division of

Serving persecuted Christians since 1967

vom.org

WHOM SHALL I FEAR?

366 SCRIPTURES FOR FOLLOWING
CHRIST AND FACING PERSECUTION

VOMBOOKS
The Voice of the Martyrs

Whom Shall I Fear?
366 Scriptures for Following Christ and Facing Persecution

VOM Books
A division of The Voice of the Martyrs
1815 SE Bison Road
Bartlesville, OK 74006

Written by The Voice of the Martyrs with Mikal Keefer

Edited by Ethel Gould

Interior design and layout by Genesis Group

ISBN 978-0-88264-221-5 (hardcover)
ISBN 978-0-88264-224-6 (ebook)
ISBN 978-0-88264-225-3 (audiobook)

Library of Congress Control Number: 2022939978

While all the events in this account are factual, some names and identifying details have been changed for security purposes.

Printed in South Korea

202202p003a1

Contents

Introduction

*Man doesn't live only on bread. He lives on the Word of God,
and I have words from God that I don't have to be afraid.*

Richard Wurmbrand,
to the secret police when he was abducted

Pastor Richard Wurmbrand was abducted by Romanian secret police while walking to church on leap day (February 29) in 1948. When he was detained, his mind immediately went to the Word of God. Just days before his arrest, he had read that there were 366 passages of Scripture conveying the message "Do not fear." Richard and his wife, Sabina, knew that their bold and faithful witness for Christ could lead to their arrest, imprisonment, or even death under the Romanian Communist government. So the couple was reading and memorizing—

internalizing—God's Word to combat the fear that churned in their hearts and minds as they witnessed for Christ under the Communists.

God's Word sustained Richard through a total of fourteen years in prison. It also sustained Sabina through those lonely years without her husband and three years of her own imprisonment and forced labor.

Following Richard's release from prison in 1964, two Christian organizations paid Romania's Communist government a ransom of $10,000—more than five times the standard price for a political prisoner—to allow him and his family to leave the country.

Before leaving Romania, however, the secret police let Richard know that he still had reason to fear. "Your passport is ready," they told him. "You can go when you like and where you like and preach as much as you wish. But don't speak against us. Keep to the gospel. Otherwise, you will be silenced for good. We can hire a gangster who'll do it [kill you] for $1,000, or we can bring you back, as we've done with other traitors."

Richard knew their threats were real. He had once shared a cell with an Orthodox bishop who had been kidnapped in Austria and returned to Romania. And he knew of other Romanians who had been kidnapped from Italy and Paris.

The secret police had also threatened to destroy Richard's character by spreading a story about a moral failing or sin from his youth. "The Westerners—especially Americans—are very easily deceived," they told him.

When Richard and Sabina left their homeland, the secret police were confident the brainwashing Richard underwent during his imprisonment would motivate him to stay quiet about his suffering. Many prisoners who had endured the same sufferings had remained silent after leaving Romania. Some had even praised Communism despite the torture they received from the Communists. So the Romanian authorities were confident that Richard would remain silent too.

But Richard did not remain silent because he refused to give in to fear.

As Richard and Sabina traveled the world telling their story, they were often asked about the 366 "Do not fear" verses in the Bible. Did Richard have that list? While he never wrote down the list of Scripture passages, his journals and letters indicate that he continued to think about the 366 Bible verses. Reading and internalizing these Scripture passages never left him, and Richard often wrote "366" in parentheses in his journals next to the passages that inspired him.

In *Whom Shall I Fear? 366 Scriptures for Following Christ and Facing Persecution*, you will engage with 366 Scripture passages provided in the spirit that drove Richard and Sabina to read, memorize, and internalize God's Word. These Scriptures enabled them to overcome fear while serving as God's witnesses in Romania and around the world. A simple Bible search may indicate that there are not 366 passages that say "fear not" or "do not be afraid." However, God's Word includes truths that, as we internalize them, should lead biblical disciples to press on in obedience to Christ and the Great Commission as we overcome fear.

These passages have been categorized into twelve sections. The sections will help you focus on God's nature and character while taking inspiration from Richard and Sabina Wurmbrand and our persecuted brothers and sisters in Christ. Each daily entry includes a passage of Scripture, usually followed by a prayer, reflection, question, call to action, or brief story to help you connect the Scripture to your own life. You are encouraged to read and reread each Scripture passage and reflect on it as the Lord guides you. Some entries include the Scripture passage only, providing you the opportunity for a more open-ended reflection.

Each of the twelve sections includes two longer stories about our persecuted Christian brothers and sisters and how they exemplify the section topic, living obediently despite the fear they certainly experience.

Interspersed throughout the book are additional notes and quotes from Pastor Wurmbrand's journals and persecuted Christians throughout church history.

Whom Shall I Fear? invites you to encounter God's Word daily and be assured that *this* day, God will meet you at the point of your fear. He will strengthen and encourage you as you fix your eyes on Christ and live as His bold witness wherever God has placed you.

THE VOICE OF THE MARTYRS

Fearing God:
One Acceptable Fear

Some phrases in the Bible can be confusing. "Fearing God" is toward the top of that list.

To fear God doesn't mean shivering in terror when you stand before God. Instead, to fear God means to give God the reverence and respect he deserves. It's seeing clearly that God's authority in your life rises far above any other authority that lays claim to your actions and attitudes.

To fear God is to be in awe of him. To obey him in all things at all times—regardless of the consequences.

When biblical disciples face the bloody machetes of their accusers and still refuse to deny Christ, they are fearing God. When biblical disciples live with integrity and refuse to lie to cover a mistake, they fear God.

Richard Wurmbrand wrote about a sister named Nijole, who was arrested, tried, and sentenced to prison—and later deported to Siberia in the 1970s—for her Christian activity in Communist Soviet Lithuania. Her fear of the Lord freed her to say the following words when she was in court:

> Truth needs no defense because it is all-powerful and unconquerable. Only deceit and lies, being powerless before truth, need weapons, soldiers, and prisons to prolong their infamous rule for a while. A partial government digs its own grave. I am on the right side and am ready to lose liberty for truth. I will give gladly even my life.... Without fearing prisons, we [Christians] have to condemn all actions, which lead to injustice and humiliation. We must distinguish what is written by men from what is commanded by God. We owe to Caesar only what remains after having given to God what is his due. *The most important thing in life is to free heart and mind from fear because yielding to evil is the greatest sin.* (emphasis added)
>
> This is the happiest day of my life. I am tried for the cause of truth and love toward men. What cause could be more important? I have an enviable fate, a glorious destiny. My condemnation will be my triumph....
>
> How could I not rejoice when God Almighty has promised that light will overcome darkness and truth will overcome error and lies. May God give us the assurance that his last judgment will be favorable to all of us. I will ask this in prayer for you every day of my life.... We must condemn

evil, but we must love the man, even the one in error. This you can learn only at the school of Jesus Christ, who is the only truth for all, the only way, and the only life. Good Jesus, your kingdom come into our souls.

When you place your confidence in God, rather than letting fear of man or circumstance dictate your decisions, you're fearing God. You're worshiping him through faithful obedience and living as a citizen of heaven while you're still planted firmly on earth.

When you follow Jesus, there's no need to be afraid of your Father. He loves you and, through Jesus, has accepted you into his family. You're always welcome at his table.

Biblical disciples are in awe of the God of the universe—they live their lives with his glory in view always.

DAY 1

Matthew 10:16–17, 19–20, 28

"Behold, I am sending you out as sheep in the midst of wolves, so be wise as serpents and innocent as doves. Beware of men, for they will deliver you over to courts and flog you in their synagogues. When they deliver you over, do not be anxious how you are to speak or what you are to say, for what you are to say will be given to you in that hour. For it is not you who speak, but the Spirit of your Father speaking through you. And do not fear those who kill the body but cannot kill the soul. Rather fear him who can destroy both soul and body in hell."

When faced with persecution, Christians in hostile areas and re-stricted nations must choose: Do they respect and obey their captors or their Creator? Do they fear those who may take their earthly lives or the One who gives eternal life? The choice birthed by a heroic faith—for all biblical disciples, in all situations—is to fear God, not man.

DAY 2

Exodus 20:20

Moses said to the people, "Do not fear, for God
has come to test you, that the fear of him may
be before you, that you may not sin."

During his fourteen years of imprisonment, Richard Wurmbrand woke up each morning with the knowledge that he could be executed before the day ended. Yet Richard didn't fear his guards or their abuse. He knew the only thing believers should fear is failing to give God the awe he is due, so Richard daily turned his heart toward his Father. You can do the same.

WHOM SHALL I FEAR?

DAY 3

Deuteronomy 10:12–13, 20–21

*And now, Israel, what does the L*ORD *your God require of you, but to fear the L*ORD *your God, to walk in all his ways, to love him, to serve the L*ORD *your God with all your heart and with all your soul, and to keep the commandments and statutes of the L*ORD*, which I am commanding you today for your good? You shall fear the L*ORD *your God. You shall serve him and hold fast to him, and by his name you shall swear. He is your praise. He is your God, who has done for you these great and terrifying things that your eyes have seen.*

Lord, how long? How long before my love for you overwhelms my desire to seek my own way and ignore your commandments and statutes? I want my heart to be wholly yours, yet I cling to sin and self-ishness. Too often, I put myself before you. I repent of that, Lord, and give myself to your transforming power. Amen.

DAY 4

Ecclesiastes 12:13–14

*The end of the matter; all has been heard. Fear God
and keep his commandments, for this is the whole duty
of man. For God will bring every deed into judgment,
with every secret thing, whether good or evil.*

Why do we quickly do things for the people we love when they ask us, yet we're slow to obey God? Is it because we haven't yet fully felt the depth of his love for us—or learned how deeply we can love him in return? Today, tell God you love him. Then ask: What would he have you do?

> We instructed Christians to join the secret police and put on the most hated and despised uniform in our country, so they could report the activities of the secret police to the Underground Church. Several brethren of the Underground Church did this, keeping their faith hidden. It was difficult for them to be despised by family and friends for wearing the Communist uniform and not reveal their true mission. Yet they did, so great was their love for Christ.
>
> Richard Wurmbrand

DAY 5

Psalm 111:10

The fear of the LORD is the beginning of wisdom;
all those who practice it have a good under-
standing. His praise endures forever!

The woman and her daughter planned to go to the village where her son was beaten to death after they completed their training. He was killed because he carried the gospel to the people living on the remote Indonesian island. "Are you not afraid to die?" a visitor to their training center asked. The women seemed confused by the question as if it was something they had not thought of before.

"Why should I be afraid to die?" the son's mother answered simply. To her, death was not an obstacle or punishment, but merely a doorway into the eternal presence of God. When biblical disciples fear the Lord—and practice that reverence—their lives reflect wisdom and understanding in what God calls them to do.

DAY 6

James 4:4–10

Do you not know that friendship with the world is enmity with God? Therefore whoever wishes to be a friend of the world makes himself an enemy of God. Or do you suppose it is to no purpose that the Scripture says, "He yearns jealously over the spirit that he has made to dwell in us"? But he gives more grace. Therefore it says, "God opposes the proud but gives grace to the humble." Submit yourselves therefore to God. Resist the devil, and he will flee from you. Draw near to God, and he will draw near to you. Cleanse your hands, you sinners, and purify your hearts, you double-minded. Be wretched and mourn and weep. Let your laughter be turned to mourning and your joy to gloom. Humble yourselves before the Lord, and he will exalt you.

What does submitting yourself to God in this season of your life look like? Tell God—and then humbly, willingly, submit.

DAY 7

Proverbs 1:5-7

*Let the wise hear and increase in learning, and the
one who understands obtain guidance, to understand
a proverb and a saying, the words of the wise and
their riddles. The fear of the LORD is the beginning of
knowledge; fools despise wisdom and instruction.*

Lord, how marvelous that you make yourself known. How gracious
you are to offer instruction. Show me ways to increase my understanding, Lord, and to nurture my love for you and your ways. Amen.

The danger lies not in the judgment of men, but in the judgment of God, not in the death of the body, but in the eternal
destruction of body and soul. Those who are still afraid of
men have no fear of God, and those who have fear of God
have ceased to be afraid of men. All preachers of the gospel
will do well to recollect this saying daily.

Dietrich Bonhoeffer, *The Cost of Discipleship*

Teaching the Illegal Gospel

As eighteen-year-old Boupha led a group of children in a Bible story one Sunday morning, her Sunday school class was interrupted by the police. "The kids were shocked and afraid," Boupha recalls. "I was also afraid because this had never happened before."

Although she'd never had problems with the police, Boupha knew Christians in Laos sometimes faced persecution. The country's Communist government attempted to control Christian activity outside the government-controlled church.

"In the past, I heard some people faced persecution as Christians," Boupha said. "I did not necessarily think it would happen to me personally, but it was in the back of my mind that those who follow Christ will face persecution."

When Boupha was fifteen years old, she began to attend church with a friend. When she observed Christians singing praise songs, reading the Bible, and worshiping God joyfully, she yearned to know the God they followed. After placing her faith in Christ, she immediately looked for ways to serve at church.

"I wanted to serve the Lord in some way," she said. "Serving the Lord is what touches my heart. I wanted to see the spiritual growth of the kids in my church to follow God's way."

Boupha soon began to teach Sunday school. And about a year later, she received a visit from three police officers who asked her questions.

Why was she teaching the children? Who gave her the materials to teach and where did she get them? "Did you know that teaching these little kids here is against the law?" they said with an edge of threat in their voices.

Scared and shaken, Boupha prayed. "Lord, please help me. Give me wisdom in this situation. Give me wisdom in answering whatever question they have."

She responded politely to the officers' initial questions and then went with them to the local police station for further questioning.

The officers wanted to know who was paying her to teach, and Boupha truthfully insisted she taught voluntarily. When they questioned Boupha about her Christian beliefs, she courageously shared the gospel with them.

"How do you know that the God you believe in is the One who created everything?" the officers demanded.

"I passionately believe that God created everything because he made me," she replied. "In the Bible, he says it clearly. The Bible states that God created the heavens and the earth and everything within it. What the eye can see and not see, he created all."

The policemen asked no further questions but took Boupha's teaching materials. She saw an opportunity and encouraged the officers to study the materials themselves. She hoped what they learned might lead them to faith in Christ.

When the officers asked Boupha to promise she'd stop teaching, she replied, "You took all the materials already, so there is no point to promise you if I will ever teach again." Satisfied she would' be unable to continue teaching without her materials, the officers let her go.

Boupha left the interrogation with a greater resolve to continue teaching children about Christ.

"I WILL NOT BACK AWAY FROM THE LORD."

"After they took me to be interrogated, my faith became stronger," she said. "It made me hold steadfast to the Lord. The police threatened that If I were to continue to teach, they would arrest me and put me in some unknown place. I would be willing to be arrested because it is my duty to teach the kids at church."

Boupha continues to serve in her church and helps lead worship as well as youth Bible studies. Although she is judged and ridiculed by her peers, Boupha is unashamed of following Christ.

"To be [humiliated] for Jesus is a good thing," she said, knowing she may face more persecution in the future.

"I am willing and open to accept persecution if it comes again," she said. "It has taught me to keep my faith in the Lord and that he is always with me. Jesus did everything for me. He did nothing wrong, yet he died for me on the cross. I will not back away from the Lord.

"The Lord would not leave me nor forsake me in any situation. I want to serve the Lord to the best of my abilities."

DAY 8

Deuteronomy 13:4

*You shall walk after the L*ORD *your God and fear
him and keep his commandments and obey his voice,
and you shall serve him and hold fast to him.*

Arrested by local police in Turkey for "insulting Islam" because he distributed Christian books, Ercan sat in a dark, musty prison cell and begged God to rescue him. God whispered to Ercan's heart, "You said you'd do anything for me. Did you mean it?" Broken before God, Ercan wept and worshiped God. He told God in his heart that he really did mean it. Ercan began to preach three hours each day in prison. He feared God more than man and kept his commandments even while imprisoned. What is one way you can demonstrate that you are in awe of God today?

DAY 9

Proverbs 3:5–8

*Trust in the L*ORD *with all your heart, and do not lean on your own understanding. In all your ways acknowledge him, and he will make straight your paths. Be not wise in your own eyes; fear the L*ORD*, and turn away from evil. It will be healing to your flesh and refreshment to your bones.*

Humble me, Lord. Burn away any pride and my insistence to lean on my own understanding which keeps me from listening to your voice and following you fully. Quell any fear that draws my eyes from you. May I trust you more than I trust myself. May I know the joy of a heart given to you and a life lived with abandon in you. Amen.

It is better to live and face trouble for the Lord and go to heaven to be in eternity with the Lord than to live in this world with sin and go to hell. Don't fear the people who destroy our body but fear the Lord.

Unga, a Christian in India whose son was martyred

DAY 10

Psalm 25:11–15

For your name's sake, O Lord, pardon my guilt, for it is great. Who is the man who fears the Lord? Him will he instruct in the way that he should choose. His soul shall abide in well-being, and his offspring shall inherit the land. The friendship of the Lord is for those who fear him, and he makes known to them his covenant. My eyes are ever toward the Lord, for he will pluck my feet out of the net.

In Communist Russia, Maria wrote to her parents from prison. Imprisoned because of her bold and faithful witness, Maria's eyes shone with the peace of God and an unearthly joy as she wrote. She communicated to her parents that though she was indeed suffering, she would continue her bold and faithful witness if freed. She wrote, "I'm glad that God loves me so much and gives me the joy to endure for his name."

As we fear God, we demonstrate that all glory belongs to his name. Praise God today for the opportunity to live for his name's sake.

DAY 11

Luke 12:4–7

"I tell you, my friends, do not fear those who kill the
body, and after that have nothing more that they can
do. But I will warn you whom to fear: fear him who,
after he has killed, has authority to cast into hell. Yes,
I tell you, fear him! Are not five sparrows sold for two
pennies? And not one of them is forgotten before God.
Why, even the hairs of your head are all numbered. Fear
not; you are of more value than many sparrows."

Richard Wurmbrand's advice to believers reflected Christ's words to his disciples. He wrote in his journal as he meditated on this passage, "Only you, my friends, don't have to be afraid of death because your sins have become white. The others have to fear." If you are a child of God, Christ's words apply to you, too. So fear not—your sins have become white!

DAY 12

Proverbs 8:12–13

I, wisdom, dwell with prudence, and I find knowledge and discretion. The fear of the LORD is hatred of evil. Pride and arrogance and the way of evil and perverted speech I hate.

How do you know if you fear God? If you find that you hate the evil God hates—pride, arrogance, deception, deceit—that is a good sign. If you long for speech that's pure, for intentions that honor God, that is another good sign. What is the state of your heart today? Are you delighting in things God hates? Confess to God those places where you need him to align your heart with his.

DAY 13

Psalm 33:18

Behold, the eye of the LORD is on those who fear him, on those who hope in his steadfast love, that he may deliver their soul from death and keep them alive in famine.

How reassuring these words must be to persecuted Christians whose suffering often goes unnoticed by the world. God has not forgotten them—and he will never forget them. Your Father is faithful to his children. He holds our souls in his mighty hand and will bring us safely into eternity with him. Let this promise give you courage.

DAY 14

Proverbs 9:10–11

The fear of the LORD is the beginning of wisdom, and the knowledge of the Holy One is insight. For by me your days will be multiplied, and years will be added to your life.

I f honoring and obeying God are where wisdom begins, how wise would you say you are? Reflect on your answer. What steps could you take to help you grow in wisdom? Journal your response below.

DAY 15

Deuteronomy 28:58

*"If you are not careful to do all the words of this law
that are written in this book, that you may fear this
glorious and awesome name, the LORD your God."*

Even while Richard Wurmbrand endured brutal treatment in prison, he feared God and praised his glorious name. He wrote: "One great lesson arose from all the beatings, tortures, and butchery of the Communists: *that the spirit is master of the body.* We felt the torture, but it often seemed as something distant and far removed from the spirit, which was lost in the glory of Christ and his presence with us."

God's name is glorious, a name above all others. We speak of God with utmost reverence not because we are afraid of him but because his glory inspires our awe. What trials are you facing, and how are you speaking of God in the midst of them?

DAY 16

Proverbs 14:26–27

In the fear of the LORD one has strong confidence,
and his children will have a refuge. The fear
of the LORD is a fountain of life, that one may
turn away from the snares of death.

Lord, when Solomon wrote this proverb, he knew the value of sweet water in a wilderness. It's essential, life-giving. You are all that and more in my life, Lord. I walk in confidence because of you. I can face my fears because of you. I praise you, Lord! Amen.

DAY 17

Psalm 34:4–5, 7, 9

*I sought the LORD, and he answered me and delivered
me from all my fears. Those who look to him are
radiant, and their faces shall never be ashamed. The
angel of the LORD encamps around those who fear
him, and delivers them. Oh, fear the LORD, you
his saints, for those who fear him have no lack!*

Richard Wurmbrand was imprisoned with a young priest. One day,
a prison officer asked the priest if he still believed in God. The
priest was quiet for a few minutes, and then his face began to shine.
The officers were awestruck by his response: "Mr. Lieutenant, when I
became a priest, I knew that thousands of priests during church history had given their life for Christ. In becoming a priest, I knew what I
was doing. And every time I entered the altar vested in those beautiful
priestly robes, I promised God: 'I now serve you in these golden vest-
ments. But when I wear the uniform of a prisoner, I will also serve you
and love you.'"

DAY 18

Proverbs 15:16

Better is a little with the fear of the LORD
than great treasure and trouble with it.

In many countries, Christians are persecuted with poverty as well as prison. Their homes are burned, and their businesses are bombed. They have nothing, yet in God, they have everything. To know and serve God is far more valuable than diamonds; the life he gives is worth any price.

Do Not Fear

By Richard Wurmbrand

L et us fulfill even the least commandments: "Do not fear."
Fear is a great foe of persecuted Christians in Communist
countries. Many fear they will have to suffer if they join the
Underground Church. In this secret work, every mistake can
be fatal. Errors in organizing an underground printing plant
or in bringing Bibles into a Communist country can result in
imprisonment, torture, and death. Therefore, some are fearful
to get involved.

Those who fear may eventually deny their Lord, like Peter.
Fear grows, like the ripple effect when a stone is tossed in the
water. The circle gets bigger and bigger.

Fear is also a decisive hindrance to Christian life in the free
world. We fear we will have to suffer in our family, in our jobs,
in our finances, if we obey a commandment of Christ. We also
fear mistakes in life, but the greatest mistake is to fear mistakes.

God's Word has to be spread, in spite of mistakes in Christian work. Tragedies might ensue, but they only underscore the
importance of spreading the Word of God.

We all have tasks from God. It is better to fulfill them with
mistakes than leave them unfulfilled. Do not fear. Our models
are Christians who have conquered fear.

It is a triumph not only to confront a terrible death for Christ's sake—but also to accept the daily affliction in our homes and places of business—to bear without complaint: poverty, sickness, or any other suffering.

It is God's commandment not to fear. We cancel the value of our sacrifices by fearing and complaining. When life leads us through the valley of the shadow of death, let us fearlessly sing some psalm, even if suffering is at its peak.

Why should we fear those who can kill us or break our hearts? Once we have passed from this life, our foes can no longer harm us. We will be with God. Why should we fear the betrayal of friends? It helps us come to the peaks of love.

We can imitate Jesus, who called Judas "Friend." Indifference is more difficult to endure than hatred and betrayal. We can make up for it by showing ardent love to the indifferent.

"THE GREATEST MISTAKE IS TO FEAR MISTAKES."

It is sheer unreasonableness for men created by a loving God and redeemed by a loving Savior to fear any man or anything that may happen. We should have a reverential fear of God, that is, we should fear to grieve him through sinning. Those who fear only God are a terror to the interests and kingdoms of darkness. Christians need not fear Communism, but rather Communists should fear us.

Fear is the greatest enemy of candor. Out of fear, many of us conform to the opinions of others instead of following our conscience. In the West, too, society demands that we be something other than what God calls us to. Persecuted Christians teach us to overcome any fear.

Let us take examples from the heroes of faith like those persecuted for Christ in Communist countries. Instead of enriching themselves at the expense of others, they enrich our lives with their beautiful witness. Let us remember them in our prayers.

DAY 19

Luke 1:46–53

And Mary said, "My soul magnifies the Lord, and my spirit rejoices in God my Savior, for he has looked on the humble estate of his servant. For behold, from now on all generations will call me blessed; for he who is mighty has done great things for me, and holy is his name. And his mercy is for those who fear him from generation to generation. He has shown strength with his arm; he has scattered the proud in the thoughts of their hearts; he has brought down the mighty from their thrones and exalted those of humble estate; he has filled the hungry with good things, and the rich he has sent away empty."

M ary had much to fear. Her pregnancy threatened to end her engagement to Joseph and leave her facing punishment for adultery. Yet even in the face of uncertain circumstances, she feared the Lord and chose to glorify God. What is your response to uncertainty in your life?

DAY 20

Psalm 147:1, 10–11

Praise the LORD! For it is good to sing praises to our God;
for it is pleasant, and a song of praise is fitting. His delight
is not in the strength of the horse, nor his pleasure in
the legs of a man, but the LORD takes pleasure in those
who fear him, in those who hope in his steadfast love.

For biblical disciples, obedience flows not from fear of punishment but from holding God in awe and reverence. We gladly give our hearts to the One who has given us life. We praise him because we can do nothing less.

DAY 21

Proverbs 16:6–7

By steadfast love and faithfulness iniquity is atoned for, and by the fear of the LORD one turns away from evil. When a man's ways please the LORD, he makes even his enemies to be at peace with him.

Stretched to the breaking point, Sabina Wurmbrand nearly succumbed to the prison interrogator's maddening methods. The interrogator intended to discover the names of other Christians—those whom she had nurtured in the Christian faith. The interrogator tried a new approach—bribery. "Everyone has his price, so why don't you name yours?" he offered. With fiery conviction, Sabina replied: "Thank you, but I have sold myself already. The Son of God was tortured and gave his life for me. Through him, I can reach heaven. Can you pay a higher price than that?"

It's not enough to hold temptation at arm's length. Honoring God requires that we turn away from what tempts us and move closer to him. How does Sabina's story inspire you to fear the Lord and turn away from evil today?

DAY 22

Malachi 3:16–17

*Then those who feared the LORD spoke with one
another. The LORD paid attention and heard them,
and a book of remembrance was written before him
of those who feared the LORD and esteemed his name.
"They shall be mine, says the LORD of hosts, in the day
when I make up my treasured possession, and I will
spare them as a man spares his son who serves him."*

A day of reckoning is coming at the judgment seat of Christ, but it's nothing to be feared by those who are in Christ. Those who walk in obedience will be lifted up as treasures by the Lord they love. No day will ever shine brighter and no hour ever tasted sweeter!

Those who fear him and meditate on his name shall be his jewels.

Richard Wurmbrand

DAY 23

Proverbs 19:23

*The fear of the LORD leads to life, and whoever has
it rests satisfied; he will not be visited by harm.*

This verse prompts biblical disciples to think with an eternal per-spective. Ultimately, we have life, no matter what happens to us in this world. Our persecuted Christian family members understand this and count the cost of their obedience. Rocio Pino, a Christian sister who lived and served in the "red zones" of Colombia, modeled this for us. Despite severe opposition from a violent guerrilla group that attempted to silence the witness of local Christians, she obediently kept the Lord's commands. She told others, "All who come here will hear about Christ." Two weeks after she boldly witnessed to one of the guerrilla's girlfriends, Rocio was shot on her doorstep.

DAY 24

Psalm 103:11, 13

*For as high as the heavens are above the earth, so
great is his steadfast love toward those who fear him.
As a father shows compassion to his children, so the
LORD shows compassion to those who fear him.*

Those who fear God have the least need to fear anything or anyone
else. That's an insight that Richard Wurmbrand's time in prison
etched onto his heart. After he was abducted off the streets of Bucharest, he sat in his cell waiting for the interrogators. He knew the questions they would ask and the answers he must give. Richard was also
well acquainted with fear, but at that moment, he felt none. "This arrest, and all that would follow, was the answer to a prayer I had made,"
he later wrote. "I did not know what strange and wonderful discoveries
lay in store for me."

God shows compassion to those who love him and who humbly
walk in obedience. Fear God, and you will find the things that frighten
you lose their grip on you.

DAY 25

Deuteronomy 6:1–2, 13, 24

"Now this is the commandment—the statutes and the rules—that the LORD your God commanded me to teach you, that you may do them in the land to which you are going over, to possess it, that you may fear the LORD your God, you and your son and your son's son, by keeping all his statutes and his commandments, which I command you, all the days of your life, and that your days may be long. It is the LORD your God you shall fear. Him you shall serve and by his name you shall swear. And the LORD commanded us to do all these statutes, to fear the LORD our God, for our good always, that he might preserve us alive, as we are this day."

God commands our obedience for our good because he is good. List ways you have seen your obedience to God result in good things in your life.

The Believer's New Identity: Who You Are in Christ

As a follower of Christ, a biblical disciple, you're not just a new, improved version of the person you once were. God hasn't rolled up his sleeves to fine-tune an attitude here or patch a character flaw there.

Rather, God has wiped the planet clean of the person you once were (2 Corinthians 5:17). He's started over, his grace transforming you into a new creation. Because that's how he sees you—new, fresh, his—and it's also how you can choose to see yourself—*in Christ*.

As a follower of Christ, sin no longer shackles you. You are forgiven and set free. You no longer stumble in fear, but boldly walk in the light.

You truly are a new creation in Christ—but do you see yourself that way?

It's a challenge when every mirror you pass sends back a reflection of the person you've always resembled: Same hair, same nose, same brow wrinkled with worry.

These are worries you no longer need to fear because of who—and whose—you are.

For Richard and Sabina, their whole lives changed when they placed their trust in Christ. Before they knew Christ, they had lived for the pleasures of this world and quarreled over trivialities. Richard wrote that he would have divorced Sabina with barely a second thought if she had interfered with his enjoyment. But Christ transformed them; they were new creatures. And they willingly suffered for Christ as they boldly witnessed for him in their homeland of Romania, first to the Nazis and then to the Russian Communists.

When fear clutches at you, does the certainty of your new life nudge it aside? Do you find peace in the promise that God's love and presence is now and forever—no matter what?

Don't let mirrors or memories deceive you. When you first found new life in Jesus, a transformation started in you—and it continues. God sees you clearly; trust his view of who you are.

His creation. His child. His pride and joy.

DAY 26

2 Corinthians 5:21

For our sake he made him to be sin who knew no sin, so
that in him we might become the righteousness of God.

Thank you, Lord, that you're transforming me, moving me from death to life, and from fear to freedom. My old self is a husk of who I am becoming in you. I praise you for the new life welling up inside me, for the gift of hope and confidence in you! Amen.

DAY 27

Romans 10:9–13

Because, if you confess with your mouth that Jesus is Lord and believe in your heart that God raised him from the dead, you will be saved. For with the heart one believes and is justified, and with the mouth one confesses and is saved. For the Scripture says, "Everyone who believes in him will not be put to shame." For there is no distinction between Jew and Greek; for the same Lord is Lord of all, bestowing his riches on all who call on him. For "everyone who calls on the name of the Lord will be saved."

Because of God's mercy, he gave you a new identity and purpose. His grace changes everything—including you! What purpose do you live for? How could your life change to better reflect the identity and purpose you have in Christ?

DAY 28

Ephesians 5:8

*For at one time you were darkness, but now you
are light in the Lord. Walk as children of light.*

Before the transformation that happens only when one trusts in Christ as Savior and Lord, each of us was darkness. That is vastly different from being encompassed by darkness, influenced by darkness, or inclined to darkness. Paul writes to Christians living in Ephesus and reminds them of the stark contrast between being darkness and light, which they witnessed each day living among the idol worshipers of their city. Our persecuted Christian family members witness boldly to those who harass, imprison and abuse them—those who are darkness. Ask God to give you courage to speak boldly on Christ's behalf today to those who are darkness.

DAY 29

1 Peter 2:9–10

But you are a chosen race, a royal priesthood, a holy nation, a people for his own possession, that you may proclaim the excellencies of him who called you out of darkness into his marvelous light. Once you were not a people, but now you are God's people; once you had not received mercy, but now you have received mercy.

Eight Christian families lived in Sonxi's small village in Communist Laos, but she had never paid much attention to them. She certainly never imagined she would become one of them. All Sonxi really noticed was that they were different from the other villagers. They didn't gossip, they were humble, and they encouraged her when she talked to them. Sonxi eventually chose to follow Jesus Christ because of the testimony of the villagers; they were God's people and shared a message of hope. Even though she was rejected by her family because of her new faith, Sonxi had a new identity in Christ.

Thank God today that, through repentance, you are in Christ.

DAY 30

1 John 3:1–2

*See what kind of love the Father has given to us, that we
should be called children of God; and so we are. The reason
why the world does not know us is that it did not know him.
Beloved, we are God's children now, and what we will be
has not yet appeared; but we know that when he appears
we shall be like him, because we shall see him as he is.*

Our persecuted Christian family has found healing and a sense
of belonging as God's children in local churches. Duhra from
Egypt was rejected by her family members simply because she was a
girl. Later on, they rejected her because she left Islam and trusted in
Christ. But when she attended a local church, that feeling of rejection
changed. "I've never sensed the meaning of having a family," she said.
"I only felt it in the church; the place where I have joy is only in the
church."

How has your local church given you a sense of family—a confir-
mation that you are God's child—and encouraged you to overcome
fear?

DAY 31

Revelation 1:5–6

To him who loves us and has freed us from
our sins by his blood and made us a kingdom,
priests to his God and Father, to him be glory
and dominion forever and ever. Amen.

In the Old Testament, the duty of priests was to represent the people before God through repeated sacrifices and burnt offerings. Because of Christ, you are no longer an outsider who wishes you could know God—you are a priest with access to him at all times. So don't feel fear or insecurity about where you stand with God. You stand in his throne room, coming to offer him praise. Offer him praise now with your words, your actions, and the cries of your heart.

DAY 32

Romans 6:17–18

*But thanks be to God, that you who were once slaves of sin
have become obedient from the heart to the standard of
teaching to which you were committed, and, having been
set free from sin, have become slaves of righteousness.*

Pastor Surjan became a believer after he was healed from the same illness that had caused the death of his seven-year-old daughter. Like most people in his Indian tribal village, he was an animist and worshiped nature through animal sacrifices and offerings of alcohol. But after Christians prayed for Surjan and he lived, Surjan gave his life to Christ. He was set free!

Lord, thank you that, through Christ, you have unshackled us from sin and made us slaves to righteousness. Because of you, we no longer have to live in fear. We no longer have to fear any idol. You have put all things right! Amen.

Becoming Paul

After completing high school, Khin Maung joined the Myanmar Army. He quickly rose to the rank of lieutenant colonel. Khin developed a reputation for brutality toward his soldiers and reserved his harshest treatment for Christians.

He took every opportunity to publicly mock and embarrass Christians in his battalion. And as cruelly as he treated his soldiers, Khin treated civilian Christians even worse, especially the ethnically Burmese who had left Buddhism for Christ.

Because of his hatred for Christians, Khin often forced pastors to get drunk to ruin their reputations. One time, he oversaw the demolition of a church. "We asked the fire department, an officer of the village, and some members of the military from our unit to help," he said. "We destroyed everything together."

Khin heard that Christians believed that Jesus was still alive, so he devised a plan to persecute Jesus if the two ever met in person. "I told Jesus, 'You need to be on guard. If I ever see you, I will shoot you,'" he recalled.

After a night of heavy drinking, Khin awoke to find his gun missing. He dutifully reported the missing weapon to his superior, who immediately accused Khin of selling the gun to a rebel army.

Three officers beat him for hours with metal rods. The beatings continued on and off for three days. By the third day, his body was so swollen and bloody he could no longer feel pain. "I wanted to die," he said.

On the third day, after his torturers left, Khin had a vision. "I could see Jesus," he said. "He was on a cross in front of me. There was also a lot of blood coming from many parts of his body, just like me. I thought, 'This can't be true.' I had goose-bumps, and I started to shake all over my body."

Soon the vision faded, and a commanding officer entered the room. The commanding officer arranged for Khin to be taken to a hospital for treatment. Then, a military tribunal sentenced him to two years in prison for selling his weapon.

> "IF JESUS IS A TRUE SAVIOR,...THEN I WILL SERVE HIM UNTIL I DIE."

Among those crammed into Khin's cell were six Christian pastors. Khin promised them, "If Jesus is a true savior, if he can save me from my suffering, then I will serve him until I die."

One of the pastors spent hours every day teaching Khin about the Bible. They developed a strong friendship that made Khin feel comfortable asking questions about the Christian faith.

Then one evening, Khin's friend died in his sleep. Shortly after his friend's death, the case against the remaining five pastors was resolved, and they were released from prison.

For two months, Khin felt completely alone in jail.

Then one day, prison officials led him to a small courtroom where he saw an old friend—the owner of a liquor store he had frequented. The man admitted to taking Khin's gun so he could go hunting. When he brought it back, the soldiers were beating Khin, so the store owner was too afraid to admit he had taken it.

The judge ordered Khin's release. "Hallelujah!" Khin cried out, giving his life to Christ at that moment.

> "THEY GAVE ME A NEW NAME: PAUL. I WAS VERY HAPPY TO GET THAT NAME."

The judge told Khin he was cleared of charges and would receive a promotion—but Khin declined the offer. "I made a promise to Jesus," he replied. "I don't want to do this anymore, even if you promote me."

Khin attended a Bible school for two years and fully submitted his life to Christ. He was transformed from a Myanmar Army officer to a soldier for Christ—one who wished to make amends with those he had persecuted.

He visited a village where he had persecuted Christians. "I apologized to the people, and they cried, hugged me, and welcomed me," he said. "It felt so good. They gave me a new name: Paul. I was very happy to get that name.

"They still call me that name today."

DAY 33

Ephesians 2:10

*For we are his workmanship, created in Christ
Jesus for good works, which God prepared
beforehand, that we should walk in them.*

Good news: you are fashioned to be an instrument of God's grace
in your world. You have a purpose and a path to walk in obedience as you give yourself to God. Never doubt your worth—you are a
representative of the Creator of the Universe. And not just a representative—through Christ, you are his child! Join your persecuted brothers
and sisters in Christ around the world by walking in purpose today as
God's workmanship. Tell others about the Good News of Jesus Christ.
Speak boldly. God has prepared you for every encounter.

DAY 34

1 Peter 2:24

He himself bore our sins in his body on the tree,
that we might die to sin and live to righteousness.
By his wounds you have been healed.

Arrested in Iran for leaving Islam and turning to Christ, Mehdi Dibaj was so sure of his identity in Christ that he shared the following with the court that eventually sentenced him to death: "I am a Christian. As a sinner, I believe Jesus has died for my sins on the cross and by his resurrection and victory over death, [he] has made me righteous in the presence of the holy God.... [The name] Jesus means Savior 'because he will save his people from their sins.' Jesus paid the penalty of our sins by his own blood and gave us a new life."

Lord, I am determined to live for you today, even if that means suffering for your name's sake. Bring to my mind one way I can live in obedience to you, even if that means suffering for you. May Mehdi's example inspire me to be bold. Amen.

DAY 35

Isaiah 51:16

And I have put my words in your mouth and covered
you in the shadow of my hand, establishing the
heavens and laying the foundations of the earth,
and saying to Zion, "You are my people."

We all have acquaintances, colleagues, friends, and family members. In some of those relationships, we engage only in shallow conversations. But in some of these relationships, we are more intimately involved. Those are "our people." That's how God views his children. He even said it: "You are my people." Many persecuted Christians are often rejected and disowned by their families and communities for trusting Christ. The knowledge that they are God's people brings them comfort and confidence. Have confidence today that God also views you as one of his people.

DAY 36

Matthew 17:5–8

*He was still speaking when, behold, a bright cloud
overshadowed them, and a voice from the cloud said,
"This is my beloved Son, with whom I am well pleased;
listen to him." When the disciples heard this, they fell on
their faces and were terrified. But Jesus came and touched
them, saying, "Rise, and have no fear." And when they
lifted up their eyes, they saw no one but Jesus only.*

When you feel anxious or isolated, shaken to the core by over-
whelming feelings of dread, know that the words of God to his
beloved Son are amplified into the heart of biblical disciples. As you
walk in faith, be encouraged by these words: *This is my beloved son and
daughter, with whom I am well pleased.*

DAY 37

1 John 5:4–5

For everyone who has been born of God overcomes the world. And this is the victory that has overcome the world—our faith. Who is it that overcomes the world except the one who believes that Jesus is the Son of God?

Navid and Shadi, an Iranian couple, know of many Christians who have gone to prison for their witness. Yet the threat of imprisonment means little compared to their burden for those who don't know Christ. Before they married, they knew of more than forty Christians arrested because of their faith. "For the people who were caught by police and arrested, their faith got stronger, and their fear was gone because they experienced prison and police, and there was no fear anymore," Shadi said.

Like Navid and Shadi, through Christ, you were born of God to overcome the world. Walk in faith and confidence in that truth today as you take the hope of the gospel to those around you. You're not alone. God is with you.

DAY 38

Romans 6:5–8, 11

For if we have been united with him in a death like his, we shall certainly be united with him in a resurrection like his. We know that our old self was crucified with him in order that the body of sin might be brought to nothing, so that we would no longer be enslaved to sin. For one who has died has been set free from sin. Now if we have died with Christ, we believe that we will also live with him. So you also must consider yourselves dead to sin and alive to God in Christ Jesus.

We are set free from sin and alive to God in Christ Jesus. These are powerful truths for biblical disciples. Hold these truths closely. They will embolden you when fear creeps into your life.

> Whoever embraces the feet of Jesus crucified, embraces also the beam of the cross. Whoever wishes to follow him has to daily take his cross. Make the cross your joyful expectation. It will become a source of blessing.
>
> Richard Wurmbrand

WHOM SHALL I FEAR?

DAY 39

John 1:12

But to all who did receive him, who believed in his name, he gave the right to become children of God, who were born, not of blood nor of the will of the flesh nor of the will of man, but of God.

N o child of God should be dismayed that he does not have the behavior of a saint; that he does not have the necessary knowledge; that he may not be acknowledged as a fellow believer by those around him," wrote Richard Wurmbrand. "He has been called 'a child of God' by the King of kings. This is enough.

"He who has given you this name will lead you through life, through its ascents and descents, even through death to the fulfilling of your high calling. Only believe that you are a child of God. The rest will come."

I praise you, Lord, for the greatest gift of all: being your child! I'm honored and humbled. Help me live today with the joy, confidence, and perspective that comes with being loved by you. Amen.

DAY 40

Galatians 2:20

*I have been crucified with Christ. It is no longer I
who live, but Christ who lives in me. And the life
I now live in the flesh I live by faith in the Son of
God, who loved me and gave himself for me.*

In a letter smuggled out of Communist Eastern Europe, Christians
wrote: "We don't pray to be better Christians, but that we may be
the only kind of Christians God means us to be: Christlike Christians,
that is, Christians who bear willingly the cross for God's glory."

Your faith in Jesus equips you to willingly bear his cross, even in the
face of fear and anxiety. If you feel either of these emotions, focus on
the truth that you have been crucified with Christ—and that includes
your fear and anxiety. Tell Christ what you feel, and then thank him
that you have been crucified with him and it is no longer you who live
but Christ who lives in you.

DAY 41

Romans 8:15–17

For you did not receive the spirit of slavery to fall back
into fear, but you have received the Spirit of adoption
as sons, by whom we cry, "Abba! Father!" The Spirit
himself bears witness with our spirit that we are children
of God, and if children, then heirs—heirs of God and
fellow heirs with Christ, provided we suffer with him
in order that we may also be glorified with him.

A pastor confessed that when his earthly father died, he immediately experienced fear. The world no longer felt safe. But when he cried out to God and asked his heavenly Father to sustain him, the pastor began to face his fear. The pastor missed his father's earthly presence, but God's loving presence was always with him. May the reality that, through Christ, you are God's son or daughter bring you comfort, confidence, and purpose.

DAY 42

Isaiah 44:2–4

*Thus says the LORD who made you, who formed you
from the womb and will help you: "Fear not, O Jacob
my servant, Jeshurun whom I have chosen. For I will
pour water on the thirsty land, and streams on the dry
ground; I will pour my Spirit upon your offspring, and
my blessing on your descendants. They shall spring up
among the grass like willows by flowing streams."*

Just as God chose to bless Jeshurun, God chooses to bless you and
breathe into you new life—a life that is fresh and fearless. He chooses to lavish you with his unchanging, unyielding love. How? By his
Spirit given to you when you received salvation in Jesus Christ. Thank
him today.

WHOM SHALL I FEAR?

DAY 43

Galatians 4:6–7

*And because you are sons, God has sent the Spirit of his Son
into our hearts, crying, "Abba! Father!" So you are no longer
a slave, but a son, and if a son, then an heir through God.*

Since her family lived in poverty, Zeba was forced to work as a servant for a wealthy Muslim family. The head of the household tried to teach her about Islam and coerce her to memorize verses from the Koran. On three occasions, Zeba refused, stating, "I am a Christian." Each time she refused, they beat her.

God doesn't stand at a distance from those he loves; he enters into our lives in the person of the Holy Spirit. Through all of those fears and frustrations you feel, he is with you as you face them. You confront them together, standing your ground together. He's with you now and forever, ready to embolden you as his witness.

From Drug Dealer to Bold Witness

When Mehfri enrolled in an Indonesian Bible school, he had no intention of studying the Bible. He was hiding from the police who were after him for selling drugs.

After a few months of school and three years of selling cocaine and ecstasy, Mehfri was arrested and jailed. A visiting pastor gave Mehfri a Bible, and Mehfri began to read it. The few lectures he had paid attention to during his time at the Bible school came back to him.

His heart softened toward the Lord. "I read Romans 10, and at that time, I confessed that Jesus is my Lord," he said. Several weeks later, his father raised the money to pay Mehfri's bail, and Mehfri returned to the Bible school—this time to study God's Word.

"I wanted to become someone God sends to share the gospel," Mehfri recalls. "When I became a student at the Bible school, my heart was not quiet because I wanted many people to know Jesus. There was a fire in my heart to share Jesus with other people."

After two years in school, Mehfri began ministry work on an island in the Philippines and served with a house church. Then he moved to Mindanao, a region in the southern Philippines known as a radical Muslim stronghold. The government ceded control to Islamists in parts of the region, and attacks on

Christians were common. "Not many people want to go there," Mehfri said, "so this challenged me."

He quickly joined a house church of three families who cared for and supported one another, working together to share the gospel with their neighbors.

"During the two years [I was there], God stayed with me and provided everything," Mehfri said. "I saw God with me completely."

He later moved to the Indonesian island of Borneo to study at another Bible school where he focused specifically on evangelism. On Fridays and Saturdays, students from the school shared the gospel with local Muslims. "I shared the gospel with many Muslim people and baptized them," said Mehfri.

He remembered how God had turned his criminal life into a witness for the kingdom and often wept with gratitude when he baptized a new believer. "I was thinking about what had happened in my life. Because how beautiful are the feet that bring these things."

"I WANTED TO BECOME SOMEONE GOD SENDS TO SHARE THE GOSPEL."

Mehfri formed friendships with students at an Islamic school and even started an anti-drug group to help them avoid the traps that had ensnared him. As he shared his anti-drug message, he also gently shared the need for salvation through Jesus Christ.

After a few months, a student asked Mehfri for help and said his friend wanted to learn more about "mercy." Mehfri followed the young man to a cemetery to meet the curious friend.

But three men waited for Mehfri. Once they arrived, they started to punch him. Mehfri considered fighting back but decided that would hurt his Christian witness.

Instead, he ran for his life.

Mehfri took shelter in a nearby church building and later returned to the Bible school where he finished his studies. He met a young woman whom he soon married. Within a few years, they had a daughter.

"I CONFESSED THAT JESUS IS MY LORD."

Mehfri and his wife shared the gospel with others, and Mehfri formed a friendship with an elementary school teacher. The man came to faith in Christ. He eagerly taught what he had learned about Christianity to his Muslim students until his superiors ordered him to stop. The teacher then focused on studying the Scriptures and leading his family members to Christ.

On a visit to the teacher's home, the man's son confronted Mehfri. "Are you the one who gave the Bible to my father?" the young man asked. When Mehfri answered in the affirmative, men wielding sticks attacked him from behind. Mehfri fled on his motorbike and sped toward home.

Since then, Mehfri has led ten people to Christ and baptized six. He has accepted persecution as part of his walk with Jesus.

"Jesus is the example, the model," said Mehfri. "So we must follow Jesus. We don't know about the future, but we must face it. We are ready to face more persecution."

DAY 44

Romans 8:31, 35–39

*What then shall we say to these things? If God is for us,
who can be against us? Who shall separate us from the love
of Christ? Shall tribulation, or distress, or persecution, or
famine, or nakedness, or danger, or sword? As it is written,
"For your sake we are being killed all the day long; we are
regarded as sheep to be slaughtered." No, in all these things
we are more than conquerors through him who loved us. For
I am sure that neither death nor life, nor angels nor rulers,
nor things present nor things to come, nor powers, nor height
nor depth, nor anything else in all creation, will be able to
separate us from the love of God in Christ Jesus our Lord.*

Who can be against you as you walk in obedience to Jesus Christ?
Know, as a biblical disciple, that God is for you!

DAY 45

2 Corinthians 10:7

Look at what is before your eyes. If anyone is confident that he is Christ's, let him remind himself that just as he is Christ's, so also are we.

Remember who you belong to. You belong to Christ, who rescued you from sin and called you into a life of fearless obedience and purpose. Before you are an employee, spouse, or parent, you are a child of God through Christ. *That's* the solid bedrock of your identity. Praise God!

WHOM SHALL I FEAR?

DAY 46

Galatians 3:25–28

*But now that faith has come, we are no longer under
a guardian, for in Christ Jesus you are all sons of God,
through faith. For as many of you as were baptized
into Christ have put on Christ. There is neither Jew
nor Greek, there is neither slave nor free, there is no
male and female, for you are all one in Christ Jesus.*

In many countries like Pakistan, Christians are treated as second-class citizens. But in the kingdom of God, there are *no* second-class citizens. Those who trust Christ stand together on an equal footing: we have all been saved by God's grace. We are one—a family united by God's endless and unyielding love.

DAY 47

Isaiah 43:4

"Because you are precious in my eyes, and
honored, and I love you, I give men in return
for you, peoples in exchange for your life."

Two years after her husband died, Tavesa trusted in Christ. She had received healing through the prayers of a Christian in her Nepali village. Leaving Hinduism for Christ did nothing to improve her earthly status, for as a widow, she was already considered cursed. In Nepal's predominantly Hindu culture, a widow has no status and is often blamed for her husband's death. When Tavesa declared her faith in Jesus Christ, her sons and daughters viewed her as worthless. "Even then I had decided to follow Christ and not turn back, no matter what my children say," she said. "Jesus gave me a new life, so this life is for him."

Precious: That is how God sees Tavesa—and how he sees you. How does hearing Tavesa's story and knowing the truth of how God sees you fuel your confidence to face what you fear in your life?

DAY 48

Romans 5:10–11

*For if while we were enemies we were reconciled to God
by the death of his Son, much more, now that we are
reconciled, shall we be saved by his life. More than that,
we also rejoice in God through our Lord Jesus Christ,
through whom we have now received reconciliation.*

As a devout Muslim working in law enforcement, Paulus made it a
point to preach Islam among Pakistan's minority Christian community, even beating Christians to coerce them to become Muslim. An
avid reader, he purchased an old book one day and was repulsed when
he realized it was the Bible. However, Paulus couldn't shake the peace
he felt whenever he read it. Soon, he connected with a pastor, and he
placed his trust in Christ. Paulus was no longer an enemy of God.

Because of Jesus, you and God are reconciled—everything that was
broken has been healed. Pray today for those in your life who need to
be reconciled to God. Ask God to reveal himself to them.

DAY 49

Galatians 5:22–25

*But the fruit of the Spirit is love, joy, peace, patience,
kindness, goodness, faithfulness, gentleness, self-
control; against such things there is no law. And
those who belong to Christ Jesus have crucified the
flesh with its passions and desires. If we live by the
Spirit, let us also keep in step with the Spirit.*

Abide in Christ, and you'll find that the Spirit shapes you, nurtures
you, and brings forth good fruit in your life. And the fruit of the
Spirit can replace the fear that springs up in your life. Draw close to
Christ, and you will find yourself stepping away from fear.

DAY 50

Colossians 1:27

To them God chose to make known how great
among the Gentiles are the riches of the glory of this
mystery, which is Christ in you, the hope of glory.

Read and re-read the verse above. Internalize the powerful message the apostle Paul wrote to the persecuted Christians in the city of Colossae. How do the words "Christ in you" encourage *you* today?

DAY 51

Hebrews 2:14–15

Since therefore the children share in flesh and blood, he himself likewise partook of the same things, that through death he might destroy the one who has the power of death, that is, the devil, and deliver all those who through fear of death were subject to lifelong slavery.

Are there any more freeing words than these? Death is vanquished! The fear of death is a needless worry. You can know, as our persecuted Christian brothers and sisters know, that physical death leads to eternal life with Christ. Hallelujah!

God's Sovereignty:
Our Supply of Hope

When your heart belongs to God, one authority reigns supreme in your life. One and only one.

Yes, there are traffic laws to obey and bosses whose opinions matter. Spouses to consider and parents to honor. But the bottom line is ever and always this: Obey God. Walk faithfully with Jesus Christ. Stay attuned to the direction of the Holy Spirit.

Live as a biblical disciple.

God reigns supreme in this universe that he created. Acknowledged or not, his power holds electrons in orbit and sends galaxies spinning out into distant darkness. He rules in all things, large and small, and his purposes cannot be thwarted.

This is the same God who set a path before you to walk. He has a plan for each of your days. And because God is sovereign—all-powerful, all-knowing, all-loving—you can trust that path and plan. You can embrace each day with confidence that all will be well as you obey God and yield to his authority.

After militant Fulani Muslims in Nigeria killed Zwandien's sister for being a Christian, Zwandien learned to rest in the sovereignty of God as he mourned her death. Turning to the book of Job for strength and comfort, this brother in Christ soon determined that he wanted to live like Job.

"We have our consolation in Jesus Christ," said Zwandien. "Whatever happens in this life, our faith in him, my salvation in him, our belief and trust in him, will always help us to overcome."

As Zwandien learned to rest in God's sovereignty, he also learned to forgive the attackers, including the man who killed his sister. It hasn't been easy, but he knows that verses like Matthew 5:44—in which Jesus instructs us to love our enemies and pray for those who persecute us—are not just words of advice.

"If I have a way of embracing [the killer] to show him love, I would, because I am sure that if God had not allowed this to happen, it wouldn't have happened," he said. "I would even use that time to tell him of the love of Jesus Christ."

Although he continues to mourn, Zwandien senses God's grace and peace in his life, which gives him hope.

"God is still alive," he said. "There is still hope. Whatever happens in this life, so long as one is still in Jesus Christ, there is always hope."

Despite what you encounter as you walk with God, walk fearlessly and with hope.

DAY 52

Genesis 3:15

"I will put enmity between you and the woman, and
between your offspring and her offspring; he shall
bruise your head, and you shall bruise his heel."

From the very beginning, God is victorious as evidenced by his words to Satan. No earthly power can stand against God. No spiritual enemy can hide. God is sovereign—he will prevail. When you walk with him, your steps are sure and your future secure. You have nothing and no one to fear.

DAY 53

Psalm 103:19

The LORD has established his throne in the heavens, and his kingdom rules over all.

Because God's kingdom rules over all, we don't have to live in fear of persecution, religious extremists, medical diagnoses, decisions by courts, or ungodly policies supported by ungodly authorities. Life is not about us anyway—it's about God and his reign and rule in all things. Our persecuted brothers and sisters in Christ are living proof of God's authority working in and through those who cry out to him.

Because God is sovereign over all, we should not be afraid. Do not fear.

DAY 54

Acts 5:38–39

*"So in the present case I tell you, keep away from
these men and let them alone, for if this plan or this
undertaking is of man, it will fail; but if it is of God,
you will not be able to overthrow them. You might even
be found opposing God!" So they took his advice.*

Many try to thwart God's plans, and all eventually fail. Even
Gamaliel, a Pharisee, noted this when Peter and the apostles
were arrested for their witness. Even now, those attempting to silence
the witness of persecuted Christians are sure to fail. God overcomes
any obstacle; his plan to proclaim his grace to all humanity will be fulfilled in his time. His power is absolute.

DAY 55

Proverbs 16:9

*The heart of man plans his way, but
the Lord establishes his steps.*

They all begin in your heart—your dreams, hopes, the plans you make for safety and success. Since they all flow from your heart, be sure God reigns there too. Invite God to know your heart and to turn it toward himself. Ask him now, writing your prayer in the space below.

DAY 56

2 Corinthians 5:1–2

*For we know that if the tent that is our earthly home
is destroyed, we have a building from God, a house not
made with hands, eternal in the heavens. For in this tent
we groan, longing to put on our heavenly dwelling.*

Your home here is but a shadow of the home waiting for you. When you enter heaven, you will do so clothed in the victory of God, and live a life unshackled from pain and fear. God, in his sovereignty, has promised a heavenly home to those who know and love Jesus; therefore, you can endure to the end.

> When I saw the burned remains of my house, I decided from that moment to put my trust in the Lord. I simply realized that God has another purpose that is greater than my loss. Praise the Lord for everything he has done. Despite everything that has happened in my life, I love Jesus.
>
> Anjore, an Ethiopian Christian whose home was destroyed by a Muslim for her family's Christian witness

DAY 57

Psalm 135:5–6

For I know that the LORD is great, and that our Lord is above all gods. Whatever the LORD pleases, he does, in heaven and on earth, in the seas and all deeps.

Dragged into a Hindu temple, a Christian named Pratik and his family had a Hindu priest begin to conduct a reconversion ceremony on them. The priest forced Pratik to kneel and then poured Hindu holy water over his head, dabbed red powder on his forehead, and ordered Pratik to eat food dedicated to a Hindu deity. Pratik spat the food on the temple floor, and the priest smashed a plate over his head.

"Jesus, help me! Help my husband!" his wife Dharmi cried out.

"Don't call to Jesus," someone scolded. "Call on the Hindu gods Rama, Krishna."

"You have to leave Christ and come to Hinduism!" they told Pratik, but he refused. The leaders labeled the family as pariahs, and the villagers were ordered to shun them.

Offer praise that our God reigns above all gods, and that our persecuted Christian family members like Pratik live that out.

WHOM SHALL I FEAR?

DAY 58

Colossians 1:18–20

*And he is the head of the body, the church. He is
the beginning, the firstborn from the dead, that in
everything he might be preeminent. For in him all the
fullness of God was pleased to dwell, and through him
to reconcile to himself all things, whether on earth or
in heaven, making peace by the blood of his cross.*

Not only is God sovereign, but so is Jesus, the Son. He's everlasting, the very fullness of God. And he chose to dwell here in the mud and misery to redeem us—to redeem you! Praise him today—he rescued you.

DAY 59

Isaiah 25:1

*O LORD, you are my God; I will exalt you; I will
praise your name, for you have done wonderful
things, plans formed of old, faithful and sure.*

Lord, your plans don't shift because of circumstances. They were
formed of old, as faithful and true then as they are now. I praise
you, Lord. I elevate your name, a name above all names. You are my
God, and I will lift you up today and forever. Amen.

DAY 60

Jeremiah 26:12–15

*Then Jeremiah spoke to all the officials and all the people, saying, "The L*ORD *sent me to prophesy against this house and this city all the words you have heard. Now therefore mend your ways and your deeds, and obey the voice of the L*ORD *your God, and the L*ORD *will relent of the disaster that he has pronounced against you. But as for me, behold, I am in your hands. Do with me as seems good and right to you. Only know for certain that if you put me to death, you will bring innocent blood upon yourselves and upon this city and its inhabitants, for in truth the L*ORD *sent me to you to speak all these words in your ears."*

No one wanted to hear from Jeremiah, yet Jeremiah knew God had commissioned him to share his message in the face of certain rejection. Jeremiah knew God was sovereign and must be obeyed—at any cost. As you face rejection for your bold witness, your obedience in the face of opposition demonstrates trust in the sovereign God to all who surround you.

DAY 61

Ephesians 1:11–14

In him we have obtained an inheritance, having been predestined according to the purpose of him who works all things according to the counsel of his will, so that we who were the first to hope in Christ might be to the praise of his glory. In him you also, when you heard the word of truth, the gospel of your salvation, and believed in him, were sealed with the promised Holy Spirit, who is the guarantee of our inheritance until we acquire possession of it, to the praise of his glory.

Our persecuted brothers and sisters in Christ who lose every earthly thing for their Christian witness don't truly lose everything. They still have hope in an unshakable certainty in their eternal inheritance. All followers of Jesus Christ have that same hope, that same certainty. Your future is sealed by God's love and the promise of the Holy Spirit.

DAY 62

Isaiah 46:8–10

"Remember this and stand firm, recall it to mind, you transgressors, remember the former things of old; for I am God, and there is no other; I am God, and there is none like me, declaring the end from the beginning and from ancient times things not yet done, saying, 'My counsel shall stand, and I will accomplish all my purpose.'"

Our persecuted Christian brothers and sisters often fear for their families when they encounter opposition to their bold witness. But when they remember that they serve a sovereign God, they stand firm. And as they stand, God accomplishes his purposes through them.

DAY 63

Romans 11:33–36

Oh, the depth of the riches and wisdom and knowledge
of God! How unsearchable are his judgments and
how inscrutable his ways! "For who has known the
mind of the Lord, or who has been his counselor?"
"Or who has given a gift to him that he might be
repaid?" For from him and through him and to him
are all things. To him be glory forever. Amen.

You are holy, God, unfathomably deep and wise. Yet you have re-vealed enough about yourself that I can see you clearly. I see your majesty on display in all creation, and your love demonstrated to a lost and dying world. Thank you, Father, for all that comes from you and through you so I can set aside fear and choose to trust you. Amen.

DAY 64

Daniel 2:21–22

*He changes times and seasons; he removes kings
and sets up kings; he gives wisdom to the wise and
knowledge to those who have understanding; he
reveals deep and hidden things; he knows what is
in the darkness, and the light dwells with him.*

The Chinese Communist Party forms an authoritarian government that seeks to control every aspect of Chinese citizens' lives.
The party's police state acts with impunity in every city and village
nationwide. Our Christian brothers and sisters' criminal acts include
simple activities of faith such as discipling children and distributing Bibles and Christian-discipleship literature. Despite the oppression and
persecution Christians endure under communism, the government has
not slowed the advance of the gospel. Ultimately, no government can
succeed in setting itself above God.

Biblical disciples need not fear darkness when they walk in God's
light. Tell God where fear darkens your path today.

DAY 65

Proverbs 19:21

Many are the plans in the mind of a man, but it is the purpose of the LORD that will stand.

An Iranian Christian, Reza, was arrested for distributing Bibles. During his time in prison, Reza realized he had not fully placed his hope in Christ. He began to see how often he had missed that target. "That was the biggest experience I got from that," Reza said. "As Christians, we can build things without having our hope in heaven. We sometimes just want to see results in this world. Usually, that destroys us and the people around us." Reza also learned to obey the frequently repeated biblical command to be unafraid. "There is a great fear when you go through this, and the Lord shows you, 'If you are with me, you must not have any fear.' That is my experience. I love that. I am grateful for that experience."

What are your plans? Place them before the Lord. How do your plans align with his plans for you?

WHOM SHALL I FEAR?

DAY 66

Philippians 2:13

*For it is God who works in you, both to will
and to work for his good pleasure.*

God works through his determined will—those things that he directs as the sovereign King of all. But he also works through his permissive will—those circumstances that he allows as the sovereign King of all. How does knowing that all things you experience are filtered through his hands help you overcome fear in different circumstances? Write about it below.

God's Unlimited Work

Shahrokh came to know Jesus Christ while struggling with drug addiction.

After overcoming that addiction and placing his trust in Jesus Christ, the former Muslim launched his own addiction-recovery group. The program walked participants through a twelve-step curriculum that acknowledged a higher power but didn't mention God or Jesus.

In Iran, where it is illegal to leave Islam, Christians like Shahrokh know that if they are caught leading Muslims to Christ they can be charged with "acting against national security," a common charge against Christians.

So when an Iranian security official suddenly summoned Shahrokh to his office to discuss his work, Shahrokh had a good idea of what awaited him.

The security official knew Shahrokh had become a Christian and wanted to prevent him from sharing his faith with others. He tried cornering Shahrokh during the interrogation, but the Holy Spirit gave Shahrokh the right words to say.

Acknowledging his role as a group leader, Shahrokh told the official that he maintained regular contact with group members as they worked to overcome their addictions. Shahrokh also reminded the official that the group was tied to a well-known international organization that was officially registered in Iran.

Hoping to anger Shahrokh, the official criticized those in the group who had come to faith in Jesus Christ. But Shahrokh wasn't intimidated. He simply replied that Jesus seemed to help Iranians who turned to him.

"If some of these people turn to Christ for help and for deliverance to help them not return to addiction, then they have not done anything wrong," Shahrokh told the security official. "You should be happy that these people in our country are no longer taking drugs."

Angry at Shahrokh's suggestion that Jesus could help those struggling with addiction, the official showed him a list of four hundred recent Christian converts in the city who were no longer addicted to drugs. But Shahrokh, who disciples eighty believers who came to know Christ through the recovery group, assured the official he didn't know those on the list or where the list came from.

"Why are you lying?" the official asked angrily. "If you and your friends have not evangelized them, then how did they become Christians?"

"I am ready to swear on the Bible with God as my witness that I am not telling a lie," Shahrokh said. "If I or my friends were in contact with these four hundred people, we would have certainly told you." Hoping to get more information so he could connect with these believers, Shahrokh challenged the official, "You give us the addresses of these people so that we can identify them and ask them how they became Christians."

Surprised by Shahrokh's boldness, the official was finally persuaded that he didn't know the people on the list. He asked

Shahrokh to help him understand who was leading so many Iranians to abandon Islam for faith in Christ.

Shahrokh gave the official an inspired response. "You cannot stop the work of God," he said. "If a person has a dream of Jesus or [if] God directly reveals himself in a vision and draws the [person] to himself, or if he has seen a miracle of Christ and follows after him, then no one is at fault here. You cannot block the divine methods God uses to meet human beings. You can close Christian social activities and house groups or put Christian workers in prison, but you cannot stop people [from] seeing dreams or visions. You cannot put Jesus Christ in prison. You cannot stop the work of the Holy Spirit. He is at work, and in different ways, he reveals the truth to people. Can you change the hearts and inner lives of people where the Lord dwells?"

"YOU CANNOT STOP THE WORK OF GOD."

Stunned by Shahrokh's testimony, which resonated of God's sovereignty, the official immediately dismissed him. Since then, Shahrokh has heard nothing more from Iranian security officials.

Shahrokh is thankful the Holy Spirit helped him respond wisely during the interrogation and that he's able to continue his work. Iranians are being freed from their addictions, and God's kingdom continues to expand throughout the country.

"Glory be to the name of the Lord," Shahrokh said, "for his wide, great, and unlimited work that takes place above the plans of the enemies and politicians."

DAY 67

Daniel 6:25–26

Then King Darius wrote to all the peoples, nations, and languages that dwell in all the earth: "...I make a decree, that in all my royal dominion people are to tremble and fear before the God of Daniel, for he is the living God, enduring forever; his kingdom shall never be destroyed, and his dominion shall be to the end."

One of the ways that God's kingdom endures as an everlasting kingdom is through the gift he gave of his Word—the Bible. On the world's most dangerous and difficult mission fields, where atheist and other governments seem to have dominion to persecute Christ's followers, the transforming power of God's Word gives hope. As you meditate on the Bible today, be encouraged that his kingdom is an everlasting kingdom.

DAY 68

Hebrews 12:28–29

*Therefore let us be grateful for receiving a king-
dom that cannot be shaken, and thus let us
offer to God acceptable worship, with reverence
and awe, for our God is a consuming fire.*

God, our consuming fire, and his unshakeable kingdom are two key—and hopeful—phrases in this verse. As you watch other kingdoms like governments, institutions, and corporations be shaken, you can take comfort knowing that you are a part of God's unshakable, eternal kingdom. And you can take comfort from knowing that God's consuming fire will one day obliterate the evil in this world for good. God's sovereign grace is sufficient. Praise Him!

DAY 69

Proverbs 21:1

The king's heart is a stream of water in the hand
of the LORD; he turns it wherever he will.

Leo was imprisoned for a year by the Chinese government for distributing Bibles. After his release, he reflected on it as "life training," a time of learning to rely on God who "will not let this training be in vain. God will show me his will for the future," he said, "and this experience will be my source of faith and my motivation to move forward."

Even in places where our Christian family members like Leo are persecuted, the Lord is in control. No matter what they—and you—may experience, it's all filtered through God's will, as he has a plan. He remains supreme and sovereign. Knowing that God is sovereign allows you to choose to walk in faith rather than fear, no matter your circumstances.

DAY 70

Luke 12:32

"Fear not, little flock, for it is your Father's
good pleasure to give you the kingdom."

The words of Jesus Christ above invite us into his kingdom—he's delighted to do so. And that new life doesn't begin in heaven; it began the moment you placed your trust in Christ. So welcome to your new home: the kingdom of God!

DAY 71

Acts 7:55

*But he [Stephen], full of the Holy Spirit, gazed
into heaven and saw the glory of God, and
Jesus standing at the right hand of God.*

Sharp stones cut Stephen's flesh and shattered his bones, driving
him to the bloodied dirt. Yet Stephen was unafraid because his eyes
were on Jesus, the glory of God. How does keeping your eyes on Jesus
help you cope with pain, loss, and fear? Ask the Lord for an opportunity to share with someone today how you stay focused on Jesus Christ.

DAY 72

Proverbs 20:24

A man's steps are from the LORD; how then
can man understand his way?

Lord, when circumstances stir uncertainty and fear, you know my frustration. That frustration leads me to attempt to control my circumstances. Forgive me. I know I have no right to those answers. Your ways are far beyond mine; your paths are always straight and true. Order the steps of all who love you, Holy One. You reign; I follow. Amen.

DAY 73

Colossians 1:15–17

He is the image of the invisible God, the firstborn of all
creation. For by him all things were created, in heaven
and on earth, visible and invisible, whether thrones
or dominions or rulers or authorities—all things were
created through him and for him. And he is before
all things, and in him all things hold together.

Fill in the blank: When it comes to my marriage, job, family, and finances, _____ holds my life together. If your answer is anything other than the Lord Jesus Christ, you are leaving room in your life for anxiety and fear.

DAY 74

Isaiah 14:24, 27

The LORD of hosts has sworn: "As I have planned, so shall it be, and as I have purposed, so shall it stand, for the LORD of hosts has purposed, and who will annul it? His hand is stretched out, and who will turn it back?"

On trial for sharing the gospel in Iran, Soro was disappointed that she had never been able to speak during a court hearing. She asked the Lord for that opportunity. She arrived at the court and began to tremble as she sensed the Holy Spirit say, "This is the day!" And to her joy, the judge agreed to let her speak. She shared boldly about Jesus, the sacrificial Lamb of God.

When she finished, the judge said, "You know, we Muslims can't be perfect all the time."

"I know," Soro replied, "neither can I. That is why we need a Savior, a sacrifice for our sins."

God plans to redeem mankind—and you're called to join him in that purpose. What part will you play in his plan today?

WHOM SHALL I FEAR?

DAY 75

1 Timothy 1:17

To the King of the ages, immortal, invisible, the only
God, be honor and glory forever and ever. Amen.

S o far, every kingdom but one has come with an expiration date.
Just one kingdom is timeless—and the Lord rules over it. The kingdom of God has no beginning and no end, and through Christ, it's your eternal home. You are blessed!

God Holds the Keys

After four days of meeting with persecuted Christians in Sudan, Petr Jasek, a Czech citizen, was headed home when an airport security officer tapped him on the shoulder. Boarding pass in hand, Petr assumed he was just getting an extra security screening at Khartoum airport.

Everything seemed routine—until the officer spread out photographs of Petr outside his hotel and at a restaurant where he'd shared a meal with a Sudanese pastor. Petr had been under surveillance since he entered the country.

He wouldn't need the boarding pass.

Falsely charged with espionage and entering Sudan illegally, Petr had known arrest and imprisonment might become part of his story. He'd even dreamt about it.

"More than two years earlier I had dreamed I was in prison, which is not that surprising considering my work with persecuted Christians," said Petr. "In that dream, I saw the door of my prison cell and heard the lock click into place. The dream affected me so much, a friend noticed the anguish on my face the next morning at church and asked me what was wrong."

Petr was taken to a Sudanese prison. The guard opened a cell door about 1:30 a.m. and Petr saw one man on a bed and five more sleeping on the floor. Petr moved carefully so he would not step on his new neighbors; Petr turned around as the guard heaved the cell door shut.

He felt sure he'd seen that door before. Then it hit him: It was the same door he'd seen in his dream. The same color, the same window cut into the middle of the door, the same ominous "click" as it bolted shut.

Petr realized his visit to the Sudanese prison was no surprise to the all-knowing God he served. His dream from two years earlier was a reminder of God's sovereign control over whatever Petr might face.

He found a sliver of space on the floor and lay down with his questions. How long would he be there? What was his family thinking? What had they been told?

The next morning, his cellmates asked for information from outside the prison. Petr told them about the November 13, 2015, ISIS attacks that killed 130 people in Paris. The men leaped to their feet and shouted, "Allahu akbar! Allahu akbar!" (Allah is great! Allah is great!) Their joy shocked and frightened Petr. He decided not to share additional information.

His cellmates became increasingly demanding, especially during the five times every day when Muslims pray. They told him to stand behind them while they prayed so their eyes wouldn't fall on a Christian. Then they ordered him to stand in the bathroom. Finally, they ordered him to face the toilet and not even turn toward them.

In time his cellmates began calling him "filthy pig." They hit him with a broom handle and eventually punched and kicked him. Despite the abuse, Petr realized God was performing a miracle. He experienced peace. God was with him.

Petr dedicated his prison time to the Lord. "If you give me opportunities to share the gospel, I will stay here as long as you want," Petr prayed. His jailers moved Petr to another cell and then to a different prison as his cellmates escalated their violence against him.

He experienced a radical change of heart and no longer agonized about his trial or how long he would be in prison. Petr eventually stopped praying to be released. Instead, he focused on the people God placed in his path each day.

An embassy official from the Czech Republic visited Petr and gave him a Czech Bible. After almost five months without God's Word, Petr dove into the scripture. He read through the entire Bible in three weeks.

> "IF YOU GIVE ME OPPORTUNITIES TO SHARE THE GOSPEL, I WILL STAY HERE AS LONG AS YOU WANT."

Found guilty of each fraudulent charge, Petr was sentenced to more than twenty years in prison. But after 445 long and painful days, the prison commander told Petr he was released.

In Petr's first letter from prison, he'd encouraged his family with these words: "Please be strong in the Lord and trust him that he is in control. He is the one that has the keys for my cell."

It was true. And God chose to use those keys and set Petr free.

Petr gave his life to Christ when he was fifteen years old. He says that after God spared him from a life sentence in jail, his prayer, "Lord, the rest of my life is yours; it is in your hands. Here I am. I want to serve you for the rest of my life," carried more meaning for him.

DAY 76

Isaiah 6:1–3

In the year that King Uzziah died I saw the Lord sitting upon a throne, high and lifted up; and the train of his robe filled the temple. Above him stood the seraphim. Each had six wings: with two he covered his face, and with two he covered his feet, and with two he flew. And one called to another and said: "Holy, holy, holy is the LORD of hosts; the whole earth is full of his glory!"

Next time you feel fear, picture God on his seat of power. Seraphim hover above him, and a crowd of faithful witnesses—too many to count—sings His praises. Then realize that he is gazing at you, his beloved, fully aware of your distress. Do you feel your fear slipping away?

DAY 77

Job 42:1–2

*Then Job answered the Lord and said: "I know that you can
do all things, and that no purpose of yours can be thwarted."*

Lord, my plans change constantly. Sometimes it seems nothing I
set out to do actually happens, but your purpose is always accomplished. No one can thwart you, Lord. No one can divert or distract
you or cause you to stumble. How thankful I am to belong to you,
Lord. Amen.

DAY 78

Revelation 19:6

*Then I heard what seemed to be the voice of a great
multitude, like the roar of many waters and like the
sound of mighty peals of thunder, crying out, "Hallelujah!
For the Lord our God the Almighty reigns."*

What's causing you confusion today? Confess out loud any fear
that masquerades as confusion. Name it. Be specific. And then
confess this truth over each of those fears: "The Lord our God the
Almighty reigns." He is King—and you can walk in freedom from fear.

DAY 79

Daniel 7:14

And to him was given dominion and glory and a kingdom,
that all peoples, nations, and languages should serve him;
his dominion is an everlasting dominion, which shall not
pass away, and his kingdom one that shall not be destroyed.

All peoples. All nations. All languages. God's kingdom isn't piecemeal or a work in progress. No corner of the globe exists beyond his reign, no inch of your life outside his dominion. So serve him wholeheartedly, as a child serves a loving Father, and as a servant obeys a mighty King.

DAY 80

John 1:3–5

*All things were made through him, and without him
was not anything made that was made. In him was life,
and the life was the light of men. The light shines in
the darkness, and the darkness has not overcome it.*

How do we know that God is sovereign? All things were made through him. He is the light of men. Nothing can overcome his light. Use the space below to write a prayer of praise to God that the darkness—the evil in the world—cannot overcome the light.

DAY 81

Revelation 6:10

They cried out with a loud voice, "O Sovereign Lord,
holy and true, how long before you will judge and
avenge our blood on those who dwell on the earth?"

John wrote about the martyrs whose blood was shed for God's Word and because of their witness for Jesus Christ. They cried out to God for his justice. Since God is sovereign, holy, and true, he has the authority to judge and avenge. How does knowing that God is the ultimate judge and avenger make you feel? Pray and ask God to help you trade in your fear for the security of God's justice.

DAY 82

Daniel 4:3

How great are his signs, how mighty his wonders!
His kingdom is an everlasting kingdom, and his
dominion endures from generation to generation.

Where do you see signs of God working in your life? Write them down below, and then be intentional in telling someone about them today.

_____

_____

_____

_____

_____

DAY 83

Hebrews 13:8

Jesus Christ is the same yesterday and today and forever.

Lord, this world seems to twist and turn in a thousand ways, many of them false and misleading; loyalties shift, and opinions change. Lies parade as truth; the truth is lost in the roar of shouting voices. Yet you never change. You are eternally righteous, true, loving and just. I praise you, Lord. I give you my life. Amen.

God's Love, Mercy, and Peace: Ready Companions

When the Secret Police shoved Richard Wurmbrand into a cell, they took everything from him: his papers, money, belt, shoelaces—even his name.

"From now on," warned an official, "you are Vasile Georgescu."

As he stood in his cell, Richard knew he had been erased. His world was reduced to two plank beds and a bucket in the corner. No one knew where he was or even if he was dead or alive.

Lowering himself onto one hard bed, he looked at the other one. There was room for two in this cement and steel cage. Richard could choose who would be his companion: his fear or God's love.

He chose God's love.

It's tempting to think of Richard as a spiritual giant who was somehow immune to fear. But what banished fear from his cell wasn't any spiritual superpower. It was trust—trust in a loving God who had promised to be with Richard no matter what. As he waited for an interrogation he was unsure he'd survive, Richard clung to the promise that God would be with him, and he held fast to God's love.

You've received the same promise. Like Richard, you know that nothing can separate you from the love of God.

But, like Richard, do you trust that promise is true?

When shadows gather close, and the drumbeat of fear grows louder in your heart, does the love of God nudge that fear aside? Do you find peace in the promise that God's love, mercy, and peace are now and forever available to you—no matter what?

Who have you chosen for your companion: your fear or God's love?

DAY 84

Psalm 52:8–9

*But I am like a green olive tree in the house of God. I
trust in the steadfast love of God forever and ever. I will
thank you forever, because you have done it. I will wait
for your name, for it is good, in the presence of the godly.*

What fears have a foothold in your life?
Lord, your love is a rock, a steadfast shelter when fear rattles
my foundation and pulls my eyes away from you. I give you the areas
of my life where fear has a foothold. I give them to you, Lord. I choose
to trust and obey you. Amen.

DAY 85

John 3:16–17

"For God so loved the world, that he gave his only Son, that whoever believes in him should not perish but have eternal life. For God did not send his Son into the world to condemn the world, but in order that the world might be saved through him."

Days before his execution, Reza, a convicted murderer in Iran, placed his faith in Christ after a fellow inmate shared the gospel with him. Soon after, Reza's brother, a Muslim, came to visit him one last time. Reza told him confidently: "I am no longer afraid of death. I know that the Lord Jesus Christ has accepted me and that I am going to be with him."

When you enter God's presence, you arrive fully known, loved, and—because of Jesus—forgiven. No hint of condemnation waits for you or doubt about your welcome. God's love is bigger than your sin, deeper than your fear, and stronger than death itself. You have been set free to walk obediently and boldly!

DAY 86

Ephesians 2:4–9

But God, being rich in mercy, because of the great love
with which he loved us, even when we were dead in
our trespasses, made us alive together with Christ—by
grace you have been saved—and raised us up with him
and seated us with him in the heavenly places in Christ
Jesus, so that in the coming ages he might show the
immeasurable riches of his grace in kindness toward us
in Christ Jesus. For by grace you have been saved through
faith. And this is not your own doing; it is the gift of
God, not a result of works, so that no one may boast.

Lord, your mercy knows no limits. It stretches from horizon to horizon, opening prisoners' hearts to set them free. How can I thank you? What can I say that praises you enough? Please accept my words. My obedience declares my praise of you. Where you lead, I will follow, Lord. What you say, I will do. You have rescued me from death, and I give this new life to you. I praise you, merciful Lord! I lift you high! Amen.

DAY 87

Romans 8:31–32, 35–39

If God is for us, who can be against us? He who did not spare his own Son but gave him up for us all, how will he not also with him graciously give us all things? Who shall separate us from the love of Christ? Shall tribulation, or distress, or persecution, or famine, or nakedness, or danger, or sword? As it is written, "For your sake we are being killed all the day long; we are regarded as sheep to be slaughtered." No, in all these things we are more than conquerors through him who loved us. For I am sure that neither death nor life, nor angels nor rulers, nor things present nor things to come, nor powers, nor height nor depth, nor anything else in all creation, will be able to separate us from the love of God in Christ Jesus our Lord.

How might you live if the truth of God's unconditional love and acceptance of you guided you in your decisions today? What insecurity, doubt, or anxiety would you overcome? What might you choose to say? To do? To be?

WHOM SHALL I FEAR?

DAY 88

1 John 3:16

By this we know love, that he laid down his life for us,
and we ought to lay down our lives for the brothers.

Jesus, you revealed the way to love as God loves. You laid down your life for me and freed me to give my life to you. Help me lay down my life for others. Pull my attention away from myself, and lift my eyes so I can see my brothers and sisters in need.

Help me love them as you've loved me. Amen.

DAY 89

Psalm 94:17–19

If the LORD had not been my help, my soul would soon have lived in the land of silence. When I thought, "My foot slips," your steadfast love, O LORD, held me up. When the cares of my heart are many, your consolations cheer my soul.

Think of a time you feared the Lord might have forgotten you. Perhaps you felt discouraged and forgotten by him. Write below how he made himself known to you, even in the silence or moments of doubt.

_____

_____

_____

_____

_____

DAY 90

1 John 4:15–16, 18

Anyone who does not love does not know God, because
God is love. In this the love of God was made manifest
among us, that God sent his only Son into the world,
so that we might live through him. In this is love,
not that we have loved God but that he loved us and
sent his Son to be the propitiation for our sins.

A Communist woman in the Soviet Union found some Bible verses in a yoga book. Though she had never read the Bible, she recited the words as if they were just another spiritual exercise. Eventually, God revealed to her the depths of his love for her in Christ. "I understood God's love to be so great that Jesus was crucified for me," she said.

Let this passage sink deeply into your heart and mind. Embrace the perfect, sacrificial love of God displayed on the cross through Christ his Son. This is the kind of love that sends loneliness and isolation packing.

DAY 91

Isaiah 12:2

Behold, God is my salvation; I will trust, and will
not be afraid; for the LORD GOD is my strength
and my song, and he has become my salvation.

Aisha grew up Fulani, a predominantly Muslim nomadic tribe from West Africa. She learned to trust in her own efforts to save her. When she learned about Christ, she knew he offered something different. "I had never heard of salvation before in Islam," she said. "There's nothing like that. Your salvation is only by your good deeds—there is no assurance."

God doesn't just offer salvation—He is salvation. He is mercy. Jesus Christ died and rose again so that you can know salvation. As you trust in him and his love for you, fear fades. Anxiety loses its grip on you. Pause now to thank God for the transforming, energizing power of his love in your life!

DAY 92

John 10:10

*"The thief comes only to steal and kill and destroy. I
came that they may have life and have it abundantly."*

The absolutes in this verse are striking. The thief (Satan) is categorized as one who steals, kills, and destroys—but the oft-
overlooked word is "only." Destruction is Satan's motive and aim 100
percent of the time. Conversely, Jesus Christ "only" (implied) comes to
give abundant life because of his great mercy for us.

DAY 93

Daniel 12:1

*"At that time shall arise Michael, the great prince who
has charge of your people. And there shall be a time of
trouble, such as never has been since there was a nation till
that time. But at that time your people shall be delivered,
everyone whose name shall be found written in the book."*

Richard Wurmbrand didn't fear his greatest times of trouble be-cause he believed they could also be times of deliverance. Carry
that truth with you the next time you experience anxiety. Yes, the situ-ation is troubling, but what might God be doing in and through the
difficulties you face?

Don't fear the greatest trouble. It is the time of deliverance.
Richard Wurmbrand

DAY 94

Luke 2:10-11

And the angel said to them, "Fear not, for behold, I bring you good news of great joy that will be for all the people. For unto you is born this day in the city of David a Savior, who is Christ the Lord."

Afraid? You bet the shepherds were afraid—they were with heavenly beings! But when the angels left, the shepherds leaped into action. The shepherds confirmed the truth of the good news; then they told anyone who would listen all about Jesus' birth. Is there an action that the angels' good news prompts you to take today?

Facing Trouble, Finding Peace

For thirty-five years, Ritesh faithfully performed the Hindu *puja* (ritualistic prayer) at a temple in southern India, lighting sticks of incense, displaying colorful flowers, listening to meditative music, and worshipping Hindu idols.

Yet, as much as he longed for spiritual growth, Ritesh and his family never felt a connection with their gods. They never experienced peace.

Then a local shopkeeper, Pascal, gave Ritesh a Bible. As Ritesh read it, something stirred in him. Soon he joined Pascal at church. A few months later, Ritesh's wife, Vanya, and his children also joined them.

Pascal, who'd experienced persecution from relatives and neighbors because of his Christian faith, warned Ritesh about the cost of following Christ. "Knowing God is not so easy," he said. "You will face a lot of trouble and problems. In this village, you have to be very careful."

But Ritesh trusted the One he had given his life to—the Lord Jesus Christ—and overcame his fear. He and his family continued to attend church. They read the Bible together every morning, and the peace Ritesh had long sought came through his new relationship with the living God.

Life was different—and others noticed.

One day, men from a local Hindu temple warned Ritesh that if his family didn't return to Hinduism, they would report the family to a Hindu nationalist organization that advocated for a purely Hindu nation.

Days later, members of that group and other Hindu leaders gathered at Ritesh's house. They gave Ritesh and his family four days to reject Christianity.

One man strode into the house, and forced Ritesh to surrender his Bible, journal, and cell phone. As Ritesh stood in his doorway, he watched the angry mob leave. Ritesh noticed dozens of his neighbors stand in the distance and take in the scene.

"WE WILL KILL YOU IF YOU DON'T LEAVE JESUS."

Soon, vicious rumors about Ritesh and his family flew through the village. "The family was immoral," they said. "Ritesh was a criminal who converted his family to Christianity. Something had to be done."

So the mob returned.

Dragged to a local temple, Ritesh and his family faced ten Hindu leaders. "Who do you worship," demanded the leaders, "Jesus or the Hindu gods? Are you Hindu or Christian?"

As the family sat in silence, one of the Hindu leaders leaned closer. "We will kill you if you don't leave Jesus," he said.

Then, as their terrified children watched, the leaders beat Ritesh and Vanya. One leader slammed Ritesh's Bible to the ground. "Who gave you this? Tell us!" he insisted, but Ritesh remained silent.

After hours of harassment, the men released the family, but the leaders arrested Ritesh for the crime of sharing the gospel with his family.

As Vanya's husband sat in jail, the Hindu leaders continued to intimidate her. "They might kill Ritesh the next day," they warned. There would be no one to care for her and her three children. All she needed to do was return to Hinduism.

"No," she replied. "Whatever my husband does, we are going to follow [Christ]. We will not go back."

The police marched Ritesh out of jail, and pushed him into a waiting jeep. He knew what might come next. "I'm surrendering my life to you, Lord," he prayed. "If I die—I will die for you. If I live—I will live for you."

To the relief of Ritesh and his family, the jeep ride ended without his execution. Instead, they drove him home and questioned the entire family again about why they rejected Hinduism to become Christians.

Once more, curious villagers gathered to watch and listen to the interrogation, unaware they witnessed a powerful testimony. Ritesh and his family didn't bend, break, or betray their Lord. Rather, their faithful trust in God was on display for all to see.

Ritesh and his family eventually relocated to a new, safer home. Since Ritesh operates a rickshaw, he sometimes sees his persecutors, but he treats them with the same love Jesus gave him.

God gave Ritesh and Vanya the peace that comes for those who love God and choose faith over fear.

DAY 95

Psalm 30:1–3

I will extol you, O LORD, for you have drawn me up and have not let my foes rejoice over me. O LORD my God, I cried to you for help, and you have healed me. O LORD, you have brought up my soul from Sheol; you restored me to life from among those who go down to the pit.

Lord, your mercy reaches me no matter where I find myself. You raise me up from cesspools of sin. You restore me when I question whether I'm worth saving. You never give up on your children—those who belong to you in Christ Jesus. You never declare your children too broken to embrace. For those who need your healing today, Lord, restore their hearts, minds, and souls. Amen.

DAY 96

John 6:35, 37

Jesus said to them, "I am the bread of life; whoever comes to me shall not hunger, and whoever believes in me shall never thirst. All that the Father gives me will come to me, and whoever comes to me I will never cast out."

Never. That is how often Jesus casts aside those who come to him. Never fear that Jesus will abandon you. Never.

After Naomi's husband died, Boko Haram attacked her town in Nigeria, and she lost her home. Feeling desperate and abandoned, Naomi cried out to God, and with VOM's help, she rebuilt her life. Looking back, she realized that she was never alone. "Since the passing of my husband, God has kept me [near]," she said.

In what way does hearing Jesus' promise in today's Scripture passage settle your fears?

DAY 97

Titus 3:4–7

But when the goodness and loving kindness of God our Savior appeared, he saved us, not because of works done by us in righteousness, but according to his own mercy, by the washing of regeneration and renewal of the Holy Spirit, whom he poured out on us richly through Jesus Christ our Savior, so that being justified by his grace we might become heirs according to the hope of eternal life.

Lord, in Christ Jesus, you wash me clean. As your mercy pours over and through me, sin and shame go swirling down the drain. I stand refreshed and renewed in you, sensing the Holy Spirit at home in my heart. Only you can make me whole, Lord. Help me pursue that to which you have called me. Thank you for the gift of eternal life that only you can give, Lord. Amen.

DAY 98

Isaiah 35:4

Say to those who have an anxious heart, "Be strong; fear not! Behold, your God will come with vengeance, with the recompense of God. He will come and save you."

Have you ever found yourself in a situation where you needed rescuing? Perhaps it was a time anxiety tightened your throat because trouble lurked around the corner or your stomach was in knots because of an unknown outcome? Tell a friend the story about how you escaped and who came to your rescue. Then tell that friend how Jesus Christ rescued you from the death sentence of sin. Write down your friend's name below, and pray over that time today.

DAY 99

John 11:25

Jesus said to her, "I am the resurrection and the
life. Whoever believes in me, though he die, yet
shall he live, and everyone who lives and believes
in me shall never die. Do you believe this?"

Yes, Lord Jesus, I believe! You have conquered death and invited me
to experience eternity with you—what a gift beyond comparison!
I can rise joyfully in the morning knowing you are with me now and
forever. I can see the troubles I encounter for what they are: temporary
inconveniences. I can live and love boldly, knowing I have nothing to
fear because you are with me. I praise you, merciful Lord. You are the
giver of all that is good—including a life unchained from fear.

> I know about a child of the caretaker of a cemetery. Asked if
> she was afraid to walk through it at night, she answered, "No,
> because my home is at its end." So we know that our home is
> at the end of the road on which we pass through death.
>
> Richard Wurmbrand

DAY 100

Galatians 1:3–4

*Grace to you and peace from God our Father and
the Lord Jesus Christ, who gave himself for our
sins to deliver us from the present evil age, according to the will of our God and Father.*

Grace and peace—two gifts from God that fill the heart, soothe the
soul, and keep fear at bay. How are you experiencing God's grace
and peace today? How does recognizing his grace and peace in your life
spur you to walk boldly for him?

> My son was tortured. My daughter was also tortured.... Of
> course the body is persecuted, but inside we are getting so
> much peace.
>
> Mohammad Yousuf Bhat, a former Muslim who was
> martyred in India on July 1, 2015, for his bold witness

DAY 101

Colossians 1:13-14

He has delivered us from the domain of darkness and
transferred us to the kingdom of his beloved Son, in
whom we have redemption, the forgiveness of sins.

After zealously persecuting Christians for decades, a Myanmar Army officer named Khin made a mistake that led to his imprisonment. Through the witness of six of his cellmates who were pastors, Khin eventually trusted Christ. Now, he lives to bring others into Christ's kingdom. "The more important war I am fighting now is against the devil," he said. "[It is] the war I will fight, even though I suffer, the rest of my life." (Read his full story on page 46.)

Like Khin, when you come to faith in Christ, you no longer need to live in darkness and fear. Through his mercy, God placed you into his kingdom of light. Jesus reigns here, and you are invited to lose your life for Christ's sake. Thank God—and walk today in the light of his love. Then ask him for an opportunity to share his love and light with someone—a family member, friend, or stranger who lives in darkness.

DAY 102

Hebrews 9:27–28

And just as it is appointed for man to die once, and after that comes judgment, so Christ, having been offered once to bear the sins of many, will appear a second time, not to deal with sin but to save those who are eagerly waiting for him.

Fear not! Jesus is returning! Jot down how you feel—really feel—about his return below.

DAY 103

Psalm 6:2–3

Be gracious to me, O LORD, for I am languishing; heal me, O LORD, for my bones are troubled. My soul also is greatly troubled. But you, O LORD—how long?

David, who wrote this Psalm, asks God for mercy—now. Both David's body and soul are in pain; his suffering wears on him. During his 445-day imprisonment in the Sudan, Petr Jasek would often turn to the Lord with similar questions as he wrestled with discouragement and despair. "How long, oh Lord, will you leave me here?" he asked. "How much more can I endure?" Eventually, God changed Petr's heart, and he no longer agonized about the length of his imprisonment. He chose, instead, to focus on advancing God's kingdom inside the prison walls. (Read Petr's full story on page 100.)

In those difficult moments when you also want relief from hardship, and you fear deliverance from difficulties will never come, do as David and Petr did: Turn to God. Ask him to give you what you need. He is gracious.

DAY 104

Titus 2:11–14

For the grace of God has appeared, bringing salvation for all people, training us to renounce ungodliness and worldly passions, and to live self-controlled, upright, and godly lives in the present age, waiting for our blessed hope, the appearing of the glory of our great God and Savior Jesus Christ, who gave himself for us to redeem us from all lawlessness and to purify for himself a people for his own possession who are zealous for good works.

What "good works" are you eager to do? Jot down a few below, and then ask God for the opportunity to do them. How does living a self-controlled, upright, and godly life equip you to pursue those works that you identified? What doubt or anxiety are you experiencing as you review them? How can you take one step today toward carrying out those "good works"?

DAY 105

Leviticus 26:6

*I will give peace in the land, and you shall lie
down, and none shall make you afraid. And I
will remove harmful beasts from the land, and
the sword shall not go through your land.*

We are most vulnerable when we lie down because it is nearly
impossible to defend ourselves. Yet God promised his people a
season when they could lie down in peace—no defense needed.

That time is in your future too—in eternity when the lion will lie
down with the lamb, and there will be no fear.

Lord Jesus, thank you for the peace that will come in eternity. I pray
I experience a taste of that peace today as I do your work. Amen.

The Reason for His Peace

I am no longer afraid of death. I know that the Lord Jesus Christ has accepted me, and I am going to be with him."

Masood decided to visit his brother, Reza, in prison one last time before Reza's execution. Masood thought a family member should be there to comfort Reza as he awaited punishment for a murder conviction, and only he could handle watching Reza die.

To Masood's surprise, Reza didn't need to be comforted.

"I thought I would find him worried and upset, but he was very peaceful and greeted me with a smile and a face full of hope," said Masood. "I wanted to comfort him, but in that short time before his death, he said to me, 'Do you know the reason for my peace and strength of heart?'"

Reza had met another inmate—a pastor named Amir—who told Reza about Jesus Christ.

"Two days ago, I received new life, and I am no longer afraid of death," Reza told Masood. "I know that the Lord Jesus Christ has accepted me, and I am going to be with him—don't worry about me." Reza then urged Masood to put his faith in Jesus Christ and seek forgiveness of his sins so Masood, too, could find salvation through Jesus.

"He wanted to speak more with me," Masood said, "but the prison guard told us the time had finished. [Then] they took my brother and led him away to be executed. I saw that my brother was at peace and worshiped the Lord."

Masood soon followed his brother's example and placed his faith in Christ.

Masood often tells others the story of how he came to Christ, and the role his brother's testimony played in his decision. It's a story about Jesus, but it's also a story that shares a promise: *peace*.

> "I RECEIVED NEW LIFE, AND I AM NO LONGER AFRAID OF DEATH."

If a convicted murderer, hours from his death, can experience peace, perhaps anyone can. Those who hear Masood describe the joy in his brother's face and the life dancing in his brother's eyes during the final hours of his life wonder: *How can I have that same unshakable peace?*

Masood is happy to tell them: in Christ Jesus. That's where you will find it—the *only* place you will find it.

DAY 106

Colossians 3:15

*And let the peace of Christ rule in your hearts, to which
indeed you were called in one body. And be thankful.*

Lord Jesus, this world is hungry for peace: between nations, between races, even within families. We are fractured and afraid—chasing after our own interests and fighting for scraps. Thank you for bringing peace to those who trust you. Thank you for the certainty of a future with you. You truly are the Prince of Peace, Lord. Amen.

DAY 107

2 Corinthians 13:11

Finally, brothers, rejoice. Aim for restoration, comfort
one another, agree with one another, live in peace;
and the God of love and peace will be with you.

Notice that "live in peace" is tucked into a list of action items. Peace isn't just the absence of conflict—it's a way of embracing the world, a way to live out our obedience to Jesus Christ. We create peace because we serve a Peacemaker.

What is one thing you can do today to help other people experience peace?

DAY 108

Romans 8:5–6

*For those who live according to the flesh set their
minds on the things of the flesh, but those who live
according to the Spirit set their minds on the things
of the Spirit. For to set the mind on the flesh is death,
but to set the mind on the Spirit is life and peace.*

At 3:00 a.m. when you have given up on sleep, what thoughts come calling? An anxious list of what-ifs and if-onlys, thoughts that spiral into fear, doubt, and anxiety? Fix your mind instead on the Spirit. God's Word promises that such thoughts of him open your heart and mind to peace and life.

DAY 109

John 14:27

*Peace I leave with you; my peace I give to you. Not
as the world gives do I give to you. Let not your
hearts be troubled, neither let them be afraid.*

First-century Jews often wished each other peace (shalom) when
they greeted or bid farewell to one another. As Jesus readied his
disciples for his departure, he offered them a deeper peace—a peace
that calms troubled hearts and eases fear. Jesus offers that same peace
to you and all who love him. Shalom.

DAY 110

Matthew 11:28–30

*"Come to me, all who labor and are heavy laden, and I will
give you rest. Take my yoke upon you, and learn from me,
for I am gentle and lowly in heart, and you will find rest
for your souls. For my yoke is easy, and my burden is light."*

Ali fought alongside the Taliban in Afghanistan. But when Christ revealed himself in a dream to Ali with these words, "Come to me all who are heavy burdened, and I will give you rest," Ali felt peace. At that moment, he woke up, saying, "Lord, forgive me. You are Christ, you are God, and I believe."

What a promise, Lord! Yes, I need to find rest that's more than a quick nap. I need to rest from the inside out—to let go of the anxiety tensing my back and knotting my stomach. Please renew me as only you can do. I come to you, Lord. Please meet me in my worries and fears and carry them away. They destroy me, Lord, one thought at a time. I need you. Amen.

DAY III

Psalm 4:6, 8

There are many who say, "Who will show us some good? Lift up the light of your face upon us, O LORD!" In peace I will both lie down and sleep; for you alone, O LORD, make me dwell in safety.

What does it mean for you to dwell in safety? For some of our persecuted Christian family members living on the world's most dangerous frontier mission fields, it means avoiding gunfire and bombs intended to silence their witness. For other Christians, it means worshiping God in secret to avoid the wrath of family members angered by their faith. No matter what dwelling in safety means to you, you are called to live boldly for Christ at any cost.

DAY 112

John 10:14–15

*"I am the good shepherd. I know my own and my own
know me, just as the Father knows me and I know
the Father; and I lay down my life for the sheep."*

Sheep may not be scholars, but they study their shepherds. A flock
can know its shepherd's voice, recognize his face, and even pick
him out by scent. And that's how well Jesus wants you to know him.

How can you get to know Jesus better? Where can you start today?

DAY 113

Romans 5:1

Therefore, since we have been justified by faith, we
have peace with God through our Lord Jesus Christ.

Jesus brings peace by reconciling us with God through his death and resurrection. He is the ultimate peacemaker, the restorer of souls, the bridge we cross to enter the throne room of God.

Thank you, Lord! In you, we find a peace that passes all understanding. Because your peace encompasses our lives, we can walk in obedience to advance your purposes—even when others oppose us.

DAY 114

1 Thessalonians 5:23

*Now may the God of peace himself sanctify you completely,
and may your whole spirit and soul and body be kept
blameless at the coming of our Lord Jesus Christ.*

Of all of God's names found in the Bible, this one may be the most comforting: the God of Peace. He alone can cleanse you, and keep your spirit, body, and soul blameless. Our persecuted brothers and sisters' intimate knowledge of his peace helps them remain firm in the face of threats, imprisonment, and even death. They know the God of peace holds them securely no matter the type of opposition they face. May the God of Peace push away any insecurity you feel. He's your sanctuary, your protector, and your God. Praise him!

DAY 115

Philippians 4:6–7

Do not be anxious about anything, but in every-
thing by prayer and supplication with thanksgiving
let your requests be made known to God. And the
peace of God, which surpasses all understanding,
will guard your hearts and minds in Christ Jesus.

Paul wrote these words while chained to the wall of a dungeon. The readers of his letter were likely astonished to read the words peace and guard in the same thought. Do you feel chained to anxiety or fear? Have you asked God to have his peace guard your heart and mind? Pause now to tell God your fears. He's listening—and he cares.

DAY 116

Hebrews 13:20–21

Now may the God of peace who brought again from the dead our Lord Jesus, the great shepherd of the sheep, by the blood of the eternal covenant, equip you with everything good that you may do his will, working in us that which is pleasing in his sight, through Jesus Christ, to whom be glory forever and ever. Amen.

At the top of today's to-do list, write this: Do God's will. That's what biblical disciples do, and not because we're forced to. We obey God because we're eager to serve the God we love at any cost—the God of peace who loosens the hold fear has on us.

God's Power:
Our Source of Freedom

From the delicate swoop of a butterfly's wing to the thunder of erupting volcanos, nature reveals both God's mighty power and his artistry. In the beginning, God created, and he is Creator still.

But when we ask if God is powerful, we seldom think about nature. Rather, we think about our own strength or the strength of someone we love.

Is God powerful enough to erase the cancer? To return a friend safely from a war zone? To squeeze justice out of an unfair situation?

Our real question is this: Is God powerful enough to fix what is broken in our lives?

Richard Wurmbrand's family and friends must have asked that question when the secret police "disappeared" Richard, shoving him into a judicial system that often refused to acknowledge a person was in prison.

Was God powerful enough to fix *Richard's disappearance*? To bring Richard home? To sustain him while he was beaten, humiliated, and isolated?

The short answer: yes. After a total of fourteen years, Richard reunited with his family.

But in the moment—alone in his cell and face to face with fear—Richard confronted the same question. Could God's power set him free?

And Richard's answer was the same as any disciple's answer: God had *already* set him free.

The power of God overcomes any prison walls for those who call to him. A heart given to God remains unbound by chains. Richard's physical body may have been under the "power" and control of the Communists, but he was free in the Lord God.

God's power set Richard free, even in a prison cell.

And God stands ready to do the same for you.

DAY 117

Psalm 73:23–26

*Nevertheless, I am continually with you; you hold
my right hand. You guide me with your counsel, and
afterward you will receive me to glory. Whom have I in
heaven but you? And there is nothing on earth that I
desire besides you. My flesh and my heart may fail, but
God is the strength of my heart and my portion forever.*

Lord, there is such beauty in the word "continually." That is how
you show yourself in my life—every day, every hour, every minute!
You are there when I awake, when I drift off to sleep, through my days
and nights. I can call on your counsel to boldly advance your kingdom
while living on this earth. And I know, one day, I will spend eternity
with you in glory. I praise you for your powerful presence in my life,
Lord! Amen.

DAY 118

Ephesians 6:12–19

*For we do not wrestle against flesh and blood, but against
the rulers, against the authorities, against the cosmic powers over this present darkness, against the spiritual forces
of evil in the heavenly places. Therefore take up the whole
armor of God, that you may be able to withstand in the evil
day, and having done all, to stand firm. Stand therefore,
having fastened on the belt of truth, and having put on
the breastplate of righteousness, and, as shoes for your feet,
having put on the readiness given by the gospel of peace. In
all circumstances take up the shield of faith, with which
you can extinguish all the flaming darts of the evil one; and
take the helmet of salvation, and the sword of the Spirit,
which is the word of God, praying at all times in the Spirit,
with all prayer and supplication. To that end, keep alert
with all perseverance, making supplication for all the saints,
and also for me, that words may be given to me in opening
my mouth boldly to proclaim the mystery of the gospel.*

DAY 119

Deuteronomy 3:18, 22

*"And I commanded you at that time, saying, 'The
Lord your God has given you this land to possess. All
your men of valor shall cross over armed before your
brothers, the people of Israel. You shall not fear them,
for it is the Lord your God who fights for you.'"*

We all have a "them" we fear for some reason. Who is yours?
List them below, and then ask God for help dealing with your
"them." Commit to praying for "them." Ask the Lord to empower you
as you commit to reaching "them" with the transforming love of Christ.

_____

_____

_____

_____

DAY 120

Mark 4:39–41

And he awoke and rebuked the wind and said to the sea, "Peace! Be still!" And the wind ceased, and there was a great calm. He said to them, "Why are you so afraid? Have you still no faith?" And they were filled with great fear and said to one another, "Who then is this, that even the wind and the sea obey him?"

Answer the question Jesus asked his disciples: "Why are you so afraid?" Write down your response below.

DAY 121

Psalm 103:1-5

*Bless the LORD, O my soul, and all that is within me, bless
his holy name! Bless the LORD, O my soul, and forget not
all his benefits, who forgives all your iniquity, who heals
all your diseases, who redeems your life from the pit, who
crowns you with steadfast love and mercy, who satisfies you
with good so that your youth is renewed like the eagle's.*

Only God is powerful enough to give us all that David requests.
Forgiveness, healing, redemption, love, and satisfaction—these
are the gifts freely given by God to his disciples who choose to walk in
obedience to Jesus Christ and live boldly for his name's sake.

DAY 122

1 Samuel 2:10

*"The adversaries of the LORD shall be broken to pieces;
against them he will thunder in heaven. The LORD
will judge the ends of the earth; he will give strength
to his king and exalt the horn of his anointed."*

In the face of Communist oppression in China, one pastor wrote this
bold declaration: "[W]e testify to another, eternal world and to another, glorious King...I have no fear of any social or political power."

Those who stand against you have no chance, Lord. Your power will
shatter them, and your judgment against them is righteous and true.
But I'm not terrified of you, Holy One. I stand *with* you, redeemed by
your grace through the death and resurrection of Jesus. I'm confident
in your love, Lord, and find joy in my love for you. Amen.

DAY 123

1 Peter 1:3–5

Blessed be the God and Father of our Lord Jesus Christ!
According to his great mercy, he has caused us to be born
again to a living hope through the resurrection of Jesus
Christ from the dead, to an inheritance that is imperish-
able, undefiled, and unfading, kept in heaven for you,
who by God's power are being guarded through faith
for a salvation ready to be revealed in the last time.

Since we know God has prepared us to spend eternity with him, how can we not walk in obedience as biblical disciples, even if fear nips at our heels? God guards you in Christ. His lovingkindness shelters you.

DAY 124

2 Samuel 22:1, 32

And David spoke to the LORD the words of this song on the day when the LORD delivered him from the hand of all his enemies, and from the hand of Saul. "For who is God, but the LORD? And who is a rock, except our God?"

Carry a small stone in your pocket today—a reminder that God is your rock, the One who delivers you from all insecurity as you walk in obedience to Christ.

WHOM SHALL I FEAR?

DAY 125

Romans 16:20

The God of peace will soon crush Satan under your feet. The grace of our Lord Jesus Christ be with you.

Domiana of Egypt left Islam to follow Christ and immediately encountered opposition. Radical Muslims in her community targeted her and physically assaulted her and her son, causing her to flee her home multiple times. Yet even though she had been harassed, beaten, and forced to start over in a new country, her hope in the Lord never wavered. "Every day is better than yesterday," she said. "The Lord has been faithful to me." (Read her story on page 410.)

The wrongs of this world are no match for the power of God. If you're a disciple of Christ, his power rises up to defend you, today and forever. Tell God where you struggle with temptation and sin. Ask him to help you stand strong.

DAY 126

1 Chronicles 29:11–12

*Yours, O Lord, is the greatness and the power and the
glory and the victory and the majesty, for all that is
in the heavens and in the earth is yours. Yours is the
kingdom, O Lord, and you are exalted as head above
all. Both riches and honor come from you, and you rule
over all. In your hand are power and might, and in your
hand it is to make great and to give strength to all.*

Who is above you, Lord? No one and nothing! You alone give life, and you alone hold the universe in your mighty hands. No amount of praise is enough to fully honor your majesty; no words can adequately lift you up. Accept my obedience as praise, Lord, a gift from my grateful heart. I trust you in all things at all times. Amen.

DAY 127

Psalm 20:6–7

Now I know that the LORD saves his anointed; he will answer him from his holy heaven with the saving might of his right hand. Some trust in chariots and some in horses, but we trust in the name of the LORD our God.

Where do you turn first when you feel like life has slammed you against the wall? What "chariots and horses" do you trust for rescue? Your strengths? Your skills? Your experience? Your accomplishments? In the harshest storms, money will not save you. Neither will health, friends, or even family. God alone has the power to save you in any storm and to sustain you in any situation. Those who love God, who have come to him by grace through faith in Christ, are never beyond the reach of his saving power!

DAY 128

John 16:32–33

*"Behold, the hour is coming, indeed it has come, when
you will be scattered, each to his own home, and will
leave me alone. Yet I am not alone, for the Father is
with me. I have said these things to you, that in me you
may have peace. In the world you will have tribulation.
But take heart; I have overcome the world."*

Write down these words and place them where you will see them
often: "Take heart; I [Jesus] have overcome the world." You
know the One who said those words. When you feel insecure, know
that he loves you—he gave his life to redeem you. So take heart—as
you endure in the faith, you are in steady, loving hands.

DAY 129

Isaiah 44:8

*Fear not, nor be afraid; have I not told you from of old
and declared it? And you are my witnesses! Is there a
God besides me? There is no Rock; I know not any.*

Richard Wurmbrand watched his peers bow to the crushing weight
of Communism, some pastors even informing on church members. What might we kneel to, that in the end, will crush us or others?
And what would God have us—have you—do about it?

_____

_____

_____

_____

_____

_____

Your Prayers, Their Power

Every year, local police summoned kindergarten administrator Cheng Jie, also known as Esther, to a meeting. They warned her not to talk about Christianity at her private school in China. She knew that teaching religion to minors was illegal, so she listened respectfully to their warnings but refused to promise to heed them.

One day the police called on her at home. Unconcerned for herself, she worried for her husband, John, who had told her *he* might face arrest. A full-time Christian worker, John had given up a medical career to minister to university students. Throughout their marriage, the couple had been forced to move about once a year. Landlords would inevitably discover they hosted a house church in their home.

But the police were uninterested in John. They had come to arrest Esther for illegal business practices for her work at the kindergarten, and then she was convicted and sentenced to two years in prison. Esther and John believe the government arrested her to punish the couple for their church work. "Because John is self-employed, they couldn't find a way to arrest him," she said, "so they got me."

During Esther's two-year imprisonment, John struggled to single parent the couple's young sons, and Esther worried her boys would forget her.

Their church of about thirty people rallied around John, provided childcare, hired a lawyer for Esther, created a 24-hour prayer chain, and provided support when John struggled. The church continued to meet, even though the members were more visible targets after Esther's arrest. And church members continued John's outreach to university students—the likely cause of Esther's arrest.

"The two years were so hard," John said, "but God's grace was around me."

"OUR FAMILY FELT THE LOVE."

God's power was with Esther, too. She faced harsh conditions and ate poor food while imprisoned. Every day Esther sewed decorations on clothing. This task caused her shoulder to hurt—pain that remains with her. Life was also difficult for Esther when she wasn't sewing. Prison officials housed her with the roughest prisoners—drug dealers and murders. Why? As a Christian, they knew she could handle it, the officials explained.

When word of Esther's situation became known, she began to receive many letters—so many that prison officials complained. Esther was encouraged, knowing so many brothers and sisters were praying for her. "Thank you for the prayers," Esther said. "Our family felt the love."

After the government released Esther, she and John made the hard choice to leave China and resettle in the United States. Esther and John now live near a university and often welcome Chinese students into their home. John has led students to Christ, and when they return to China, he continues to disciple them online and over the phone.

Esther and her family went through a severe trial during her imprisonment. She sees now how God used her suffering for his purposes. "In China, no one can walk into prison to share the gospel," she said. "Pray that God can use Christian prisoners to share [the gospel with the other inmates]."

Esther and John don't know what the future holds, but they've seen God's powerful hand in each difficult moment of their lives. For now, they trust the Lord has placed them right where he wants them, near a university where they can serve Chinese students.

"GOD IS POWERFUL, AND HE CARES ABOUT US."

Recently a Chinese student from a Buddhist background expressed concern that her family would kick her out after they learned she'd become a Christian. John and Esther prayed with her and gave her some Christian literature. Several weeks later, she called John and Esther. She had explained to her family her decision to follow Christ. Her family had listened to her and accepted her decision.

"See?" Esther told her. "God is powerful, and he cares about us."

DAY 130

Matthew 21:21

*And Jesus answered them, "Truly, I say to you, if you have
faith and do not doubt, you will not only do what has been
done to the fig tree, but even if you say to this mountain,
'Be taken up and thrown into the sea,' it will happen."*

God uses his power to bring his will to pass, yet he chooses to work
through us when we have faith in him and resist doubt. Faith in
God's character unlocks in us a desire to cooperate with God in what
he wants to accomplish. Faith in God washes away doubt and fear and
prepares us to be fully obedient to do his will. Ask God how he wants
to work through your obedience today.

DAY 131

Jeremiah 32:26–27

The word of the LORD came to Jeremiah: "Behold, I am the LORD, the God of all flesh. Is anything too hard for me?"

Borila killed hundreds of Jews as a Nazi during World War II. He often boasted about murdering them with his own hands. Then Borila met Sabina Wurmbrand—a Jewish Christian whose family he had murdered. Through the love of Christ, Sabina forgave him, and in response, Borila cried out to God in repentance.

Make a list of all the things that you believe are too hard for God, including those people who you think are "unsavable." What or who did you list? Thank God that his power rules over every circumstance in your life today and can even draw the hardest of hearts to Jesus Christ.

Romans 1:16–17

*For I am not ashamed of the gospel, for it is the power
of God for salvation to everyone who believes, to the
Jew first and also to the Greek. For in it the righteousness of God is revealed from faith for faith, as
it is written, "The righteous shall live by faith."*

The power of the gospel is unparalleled. The Greek word translit-
erated in this verse as "power" is *dynamis*—the root of the word
"dynamite." God's power to save you is just as explosive. His power to
sustain you is equally indestructible. You have no reason to be ashamed
of the gospel.

DAY 133

Mark 16:2-6

*And very early on the first day of the week, when the sun
had risen, they went to the tomb. And they were saying
to one another, "Who will roll away the stone for us from
the entrance of the tomb?" And looking up, they saw
that the stone had been rolled back—it was very large.
And entering the tomb, they saw a young man sitting
on the right side, dressed in a white robe, and they were
alarmed. And he said to them, "Do not be alarmed. You
seek Jesus of Nazareth, who was crucified. He has risen;
he is not here. See the place where they laid him."*

The disciples had no idea what they would find in the garden early
that morning. But they discovered that Jesus was not there—he
had risen from the dead. God is a God of resurrection power! God's
power works in us to conquer our fear of the unknown. What unknown is causing you to fear today?

DAY 134

Revelation 1:17–18

When I saw him, I fell at his feet as though dead. But he laid his right hand on me, saying, "Fear not, I am the first and the last, and the living one. I died, and behold I am alive forevermore, and I have the keys of Death and Hades."

Read these words of Jesus spoken to the apostle John. Notice the last assurance Jesus gives: He holds the keys to death and Hades. Regardless of the evil that stalks the earth, no matter the lies that Satan spreads, no matter the earthly harm that strikes you, the ultimate victory is in the hands of Jesus.

Jesus Christ has the power to put things right! Hallelujah!

DAY 135

Psalm 68:28, 35

Summon your power, O God, the power, O God, by
which you have worked for us. Awesome is God from
his sanctuary; the God of Israel—he is the one who gives
power and strength to his people. Blessed be God!

Richard Wurmbrand wrote: "Strengthen, O God, what you have done for our family and mission." Richard knew where the power to sustain his family and ministry lay: in God. No effort on your part can ever match what the power of God can do in and through you. Ask the Lord to fill your life with his power so that you can walk in obedience to his purposes.

DAY 136

Luke 1:30–32, 34–35, 37

And the angel said to her, "Do not be afraid, Mary, for you have found favor with God. And behold, you will conceive in your womb and bear a son, and you shall call his name Jesus. He will be great and will be called the Son of the Most High….And Mary said to the angel, "How will this be, since I am a virgin?" And the angel answered her, "The Holy Spirit will come upon you, and the power of the Most High will overshadow you; therefore the child to be born will be called holy—the Son of God. For nothing will be impossible with God."

With God, nothing is impossible. No danger is too dire, no mistake too great, no calling too big, and no life too broken to be beyond his healing hand. So don't fear that your past owns you—it doesn't. In Christ, you are a new creation. When you walk with the Lord Jesus, he owns you; he can accomplish his plan as you walk in obedience to him.

DAY 137

Romans 15:13

*May the God of hope fill you with all joy and
peace in believing, so that by the power of the
Holy Spirit you may abound in hope.*

Fill a cup with water to overflowing. How is this like—or unlike—
the power of the Holy Spirit in you? Ask God to fill you to overflowing today, so that his Spirit flows over your anxiety and discouragement. Walk in obedience to all he calls you to throughout the day.

DAY 138

Psalm 27:1, 14

The LORD is my light and my salvation; whom shall I fear? The LORD is the stronghold of my life; of whom shall I be afraid? Wait for the LORD; be strong, and let your heart take courage; wait for the LORD!

David had plenty to fear—lions, bears, a roaring giant in armor, a precarious relationship with a troubled king. Likewise, persecuted Christians endure opposition for their witness from hostile governments, violent terrorists, religious extremists, and even their family members. Yet like David, they know none of what stands against them can stand against God. Our Christian brothers and sisters faithfully bear witness to Christ and live in obedience to him. And as they do, they find a stronghold in God. You can, too. Ask him for shelter today as you walk in obedience to Christ.

DAY 139

2 Corinthians 12:9–10

But he said to me, "My grace is sufficient for you, for my power is made perfect in weakness." Therefore I will boast all the more gladly of my weaknesses, so that the power of Christ may rest upon me. For the sake of Christ, then, I am content with weaknesses, insults, hardships, persecutions, and calamities. For when I am weak, then I am strong.

Lord, you know my weaknesses. You have seen me struggle, convinced that my life would be better if it held only strengths. Help me see my weaknesses for what they are: cracks through which your light shines out to other broken people. I give my weaknesses to you, Lord. Use them—and me, all of me—any way you wish. Amen.

DAY 140

Ephesians 3:20–21

Now to him who is able to do far more abundantly than all that we ask or think, according to the power at work within us, to him be glory in the church and in Christ Jesus throughout all generations, forever and ever. Amen.

Sergei Bessarab left a life of crime in Tajikistan to follow Christ. He became a bold witness as he served time in prison and later worked as a pastor. Sergei's zeal for Christ cost him his life; a radical Muslim shot and killed him in 2004. Years later, while in prison for the murder, Sergei's killer came to faith in Christ. The inmate who shared the gospel with Sergei's murderer had also been led to the Lord and discipled by Sergei.

God's power can accomplish more than anything we can imagine. And his power, working in us through his Spirit, can transform our world and point hearts toward heaven. Praise him for his power. Praise Jesus Christ for giving you purpose as you obey and serve him.

The Incomparable Prophet

Waleed grew up in a deeply Islamic family. His uncle chose Waleed, when he was still very young, to become an Islamic scholar. As Waleed grew, he became so fluent in Arabic, the language of the Quran, that he attended an Islamic university on a four-year scholarship. Following his graduation, Waleed became a sheikh and taught at a mosque.

Then a cancer diagnosis upended his comfortable life. After four surgeries, doctors told Waleed he had little hope of survival. "It came very fast," said Waleed, "and I was far from my family."

Waleed sought hope as he dug deeper into the Quran. He recognized for the first time how differently the Quran spoke about Jesus than it did the Prophet Muhammad. Sura 19, the chapter that tells the life of Jesus, described Jesus performing miracles and even being raised from the dead. "The man who does these things is powerful," Waleed decided. "He is incomparable because no other prophet written about in the Quran is doing something like that."

Waleed's interest in Jesus didn't go unnoticed by fellow Muslims who threatened to kill him. They threw stones at him in the street. As Waleed tended to his cuts and bruises, he prayed in the name of Jesus for the first time. "Jesus, if you are above and you see how I am, help me," he prayed.

The Lord led Waleed to Ethiopia, where he encountered a pastor who shared the gospel and helped Waleed study the Bible. Waleed never looked back.

More than a decade after doctors told him he would die, Waleed is healthy and serves Christ with his wife, Yasmina.

The couple works mostly with young adults. Many of them can't tell their families they are following Jesus or even that they are reevaluating Islam's teachings. These believers secretly gather for fellowship on Sunday afternoons in someone's backyard in a quiet neighborhood. They sit on cushions in the shade of a canopy, sing, pray, and discuss the Bible. For many, this is the only time they can truly be themselves and openly discuss the questions that burn within them. For those who haven't yet come to know Christ, it's an opportunity to hear a clear explanation of the gospel.

"THE MAN WHO DOES THESE THINGS IS POWERFUL."

Waleed's training as a sheikh gives him the perfect background to understand the concerns presented by Muslims and unpack the power of God's Word as he addresses those concerns.

But Waleed and Yasmina do more than teach. Since young Christian converts often face violence in Muslim-majority nations, Waleed and Yasmina have opened their home to several young men they're discipling.

The young men go to school or work during the day, but they return home to a sort of family—one where they're free to talk about the Bible and receive guidance from Waleed.

"When I came to Christ, I lost my position, my health, my job, my community, my family," said Waleed. "But God gave me double now. I am so blessed."

Life isn't simple for Waleed and Yasmina. More than once, they've had to move to a new house after becoming too well known in their neighborhood. But despite ongoing obstacles and trials, Waleed hasn't lost sight of his primary purpose in life.

"Life is very short," he said. "The only thing we have to do is to share God's power with our people, who are dying without Christ. We cannot see them and keep silent."

DAY 141

Isaiah 9:6–7

*For to us a child is born, to us a son is given; and the
government shall be upon his shoulder, and his name shall
be called Wonderful Counselor, Mighty God, Everlasting
Father, Prince of Peace. Of the increase of his government
and of peace there will be no end, on the throne of David
and over his kingdom, to establish it and to uphold it with
justice and with righteousness from this time forth and
forevermore. The zeal of the LORD of hosts will do this.*

Because our Mighty God has rescued us from death through the
life, death, and resurrection of Jesus Christ, our sin no longer
needs to consume us as we walk with our Lord.

God, guide my steps so I glorify you and serve you well. Amen.

DAY 142

Romans 8:10–11

But if Christ is in you, although the body is dead because of sin, the Spirit is life because of righteousness. If the Spirit of him who raised Jesus from the dead dwells in you, he who raised Christ Jesus from the dead will also give life to your mortal bodies through his Spirit who dwells in you.

Lord, thank you for redeeming me and for your grace which gives me new life. May I show my love to you through willing, bold obedience to Christ today. Wash away any fears that prompt me to hesitate in serving you. I want to be wholly yours. Amen.

It is only in difficulty that one sees the power of God and only in the most impossible situations does he work his miracles. We are not afraid.

Richard Wurmbrand

DAY 143

Joshua 4:21–24

*And he said to the people of Israel, "When your children
ask their fathers in times to come, 'What do these stones
mean?' then you shall let your children know, 'Israel passed
over this Jordan on dry ground.' For the L<small>ORD</small> your God
dried up the waters of the Jordan for you until you passed
over, as the L<small>ORD</small> your God did to the Red Sea, which
he dried up for us until we passed over, so that all the
peoples of the earth may know that the hand of the Lord
is mighty, that you may fear the L<small>ORD</small> your God forever."*

The people of Israel stacked stones to commemorate and remember God's power. You can also create a visible reminder of the great things God has done in your life. When others ask about it, explain all the things he has done.

DAY 144

Matthew 8:24–26

And behold, there arose a great storm on the sea, so that
the boat was being swamped by the waves; but he was
asleep. And they went and woke him, saying, "Save us,
Lord; we are perishing." And he said to them, "Why are
you afraid, O you of little faith?" Then he rose and rebuked
the winds and the sea, and there was a great calm.

An observation from Richard Wurmbrand was that few storms arise suddenly; we can often see storm clouds if we watch for them. So do not be lulled into missing or ignoring danger signs—including your fears. Those fears are a sign of a faith that needs strengthening. Your constant awareness (and reliance on God) will calm those fears.

DAY 145

Deuteronomy 10:15–18

Yet the LORD set his heart in love on your fathers and chose their offspring after them, you above all peoples, as you are this day. Circumcise therefore the foreskin of your heart, and be no longer stubborn. For the LORD your God is God of gods and Lord of lords, the great, the mighty, and the awesome God, who is not partial and takes no bribe. He executes justice for the fatherless and the widow, and loves the sojourner, giving him food and clothing.

Stubborn? You? Ask God if pride or fear is holding you back from knowing him more fully. See what he says. Write a short prayer on the lines below.

_____

_____

_____

_____

DAY 146

Revelation 11:16-17

And the twenty-four elders who sit on their thrones before
God fell on their faces and worshiped God, saying, "We give
thanks to you, Lord God Almighty, who is and who was,
for you have taken your great power and begun to reign."

Lord, I, too, give you thanks. Thank you for my life and what you are doing in it. Thank you for those in my life I love. Thank you for rescuing me from sin through the power of your forgiveness in Christ. Reign in my life, Lord. Reign over my fear. Reign over my insecurity. Reign over my doubt so that I might serve you in all of my life. Amen.

DAY 147

Isaiah 26:3–4

*You keep him in perfect peace whose mind is stayed
on you, because he trusts in you. Trust in the LORD
forever, for the LORD GOD is an everlasting rock.*

Does your trust in God continue to grow? Disciples mature over time as they stay their minds on God and walk in faith through daily sacrifice and obedience.

DAY 148

Ephesians 1:16–21

I do not cease to give thanks for you, remembering you in my prayers, that the God of our Lord Jesus Christ, the Father of glory, may give you the Spirit of wisdom and of revelation in the knowledge of him, having the eyes of your hearts enlightened, that you may know what is the hope to which he has called you, what are the riches of his glorious inheritance in the saints, and what is the immeasurable greatness of his power toward us who believe, according to the working of his great might that he worked in Christ when he raised him from the dead and seated him at his right hand in the heavenly places, far above all rule and authority and power and dominion, and above every name that is named, not only in this age but also in the one to come.

Pray through this passage today for a fellow brother or sister in Christ. Then pray through the passage for yourself.

DAY 149

Habakkuk 3:19

GOD, the Lord, is my strength; he makes my feet like
the deer's; he makes me tread on my high places.

Where are you frozen in place? Are you afraid to share the gospel and show God's love to others? God's strength can propel you to attain "high places," like surefooted deer on high mountain slopes. When God nudges you, go fearlessly—he is with you. When God aims you toward a task that may appear to have uncertain and difficult outcomes, know that nothing is uncertain with him; there is no need to worry or be anxious.

DAY 150

1 Corinthians 2:1–5

*And I, when I came to you, brothers, did not come
proclaiming to you the testimony of God with lofty
speech or wisdom. For I decided to know nothing
among you except Jesus Christ and him crucified. And
I was with you in weakness and in fear and much
trembling, and my speech and my message were not in
plausible words of wisdom, but in demonstration of
the Spirit and of power, so that your faith might not
rest in the wisdom of men but in the power of God.*

Even the apostle Paul had moments of weakness and fear. But Paul
knew the wisdom and power he received from God would sustain
him—and it did. So be like Paul: admit when you're trembling, and
rely on the power of God. Accept his strength given to you through the
Holy Spirit and from the encouragement of other believers. Lean into
God always—especially when the rest of your world wobbles with fear
and uncertainty.

DAY 151

Psalm 62:5–7

*For God alone, O my soul, wait in silence, for my hope
is from him. He only is my rock and my salvation, my
fortress; I shall not be shaken. On God rests my salvation
and my glory; my mighty rock, my refuge is God.*

Has something shaken you recently? Rattled you to your core? A diagnosis? A loss? Rejection for knowing Christ? The unknowns in tomorrow? Those whose fortress is their heavenly Father are safe behind unbreachable walls. Persecutions may come—will come—but still, hope remains. So build your life on the promises and person of your Father. His power will hold you steady when life rattles around you.

God's Presence and Provision: With Us Always

The day Romanian secret police arrested Richard Wurmbrand—February 29, 1948—he experienced a profound truth: God stood with him on both sides of his cell door.

Richard had long sensed God's presence while preaching and teaching. He knew God was with him when he told others about Christ. He had even sensed God's presence while speeding toward police headquarters.

But as his guard's footsteps echoed off down the hall and the cell's stark walls closed in on him, Richard still experienced God's presence. God had joined him in prison.

Even though he had been stripped of his belongings, Richard was unafraid of hunger or thirst. The God who had always provided for him would continue to provide—even in a Communist prison.

Experiencing God's presence gave Richard a calm that seemed wild-ly out of place in his cell. It propelled him through fear to a place of trust in the God who loved him and the God who loves you too. The God whose promise of presence and provision is iron-clad. His dis-ciples who suffer in prison because of their faith know God's presence with them is assured.

God will be present with his children. Not even prison bars can keep him out.

DAY 152

Psalm 23

The LORD is my shepherd; I shall not want. He makes me lie down in green pastures. He leads me beside still waters. He restores my soul. He leads me in paths of righteousness for his name's sake. Even though I walk through the valley of the shadow of death, I will fear no evil, for you are with me; your rod and your staff, they comfort me. You prepare a table before me in the presence of my enemies; you anoint my head with oil; my cup overflows. Surely goodness and mercy shall follow me all the days of my life, and I shall dwell in the house of the LORD forever.

Captured during the violent Cultural Revolution in Communist China (1966–1976), a Christian woman named Nien Cheng recited Psalm 23 as she walked, with her hands cuffed behind her back, to the vehicle that waited to take her to prison.

Where is your valley of the shadow of death, the place fear grips you? Tell God.

DAY 153

Deuteronomy 31:6–8

*"Be strong and courageous. Do not fear or be in dread of them, for it is the L*ORD *your God who goes with you. He will not leave you or forsake you." Then Moses summoned Joshua and said to him in the sight of all Israel, "Be strong and courageous, for you shall go with this people into the land that the L*ORD *has sworn to their fathers to give them, and you shall put them in possession of it. It is the L*ORD *who goes before you. He will be with you; he will not leave you or forsake you. Do not fear or be dismayed."*

Richard Wurmbrand endured fourteen years of interrogations and beatings—can you imagine the dread he felt at the sound of approaching footsteps? Yet Richard overcame that instinctive fear. Whoever marched toward his door, Richard knew God was already with him.

What triggers your fear? How does knowing God is with you make a difference and allow you to endure and serve him regardless of your fears?

DAY 154

Matthew 14:23–27

And after he had dismissed the crowds, he went up on the mountain by himself to pray. When evening came, he was there alone, but the boat by this time was a long way from the land, beaten by the waves, for the wind was against them. And in the fourth watch of the night he came to them, walking on the sea. But when the disciples saw him walking on the sea, they were terrified, and said, "It is a ghost!" and they cried out in fear. But immediately Jesus spoke to them, saying, "Take heart; it is I. Do not be afraid."

The presence of God sustains our imprisoned brothers and sisters in Christ when they are afraid. The certainty that he is with them strengthens their hearts and gives them peace. Let that same certainty bring you peace and embolden you too.

DAY 155

Psalm 73:28

*But for me it is good to be near God; I have made the
Lord GOD my refuge, that I may tell of all your works.*

To be near God is a decision you make daily. While facing an unknown future in a Turkish prison, Pastor Andrew Brunson despaired as he felt God's silence and absence. But Andrew chose to draw near to God despite his feelings. "I will lean into Jesus, even if I can't feel His presence," he thought.

Write down what keeps you from drawing near to God. Then list what actions you can pursue today that will help you draw nearer to him.

DAY 156

Zephaniah 3:15–17

The Lord has taken away the judgments against you;
he has cleared away your enemies. The King of Israel,
the Lord, is in your midst; you shall never again fear
evil. On that day it shall be said to Jerusalem: "Fear
not, O Zion; let not your hands grow weak. The Lord
your God is in your midst, a mighty one who will save;
he will rejoice over you with gladness; he will quiet you
by his love; he will exult over you with loud singing."

How would your world look if God cleared away all who oppose you? God could do that, but he seldom does. Instead, God walks with you to help you confront evil. He defends you when you come under attack. And he strengthens you as you choose to love those who oppose you.

Lord, I'm thankful that you're in all of those things that bring me comfort and those that cause me concern. You go before me and with me; nothing I face surprises you. I choose to trust you, Lord. And I choose to follow where you lead. Amen.

DAY 157

1 Peter 4:14, 16, 19

If you are insulted for the name of Christ, you are blessed, because the Spirit of glory and of God rests upon you. Yet if anyone suffers as a Christian, let him not be ashamed, but let him glorify God in that name. Therefore let those who suffer according to God's will entrust their souls to a faithful Creator while doing good.

When your faithfulness to God draws scorn, be unashamed and unafraid. Your obedience to the Lord Jesus glorifies him. And you're in good company: many brothers and sisters in Christ experience mockery, arrest, imprisonment, and more. You'll discover what they know: God's presence sustains those who love him!

DAY 158

2 Chronicles 20:15–17

*And he said, "Listen, all Judah and inhabitants of Jerusalem
and King Jehoshaphat: Thus says the Lord to you, 'Do
not be afraid and do not be dismayed at this great horde,
for the battle is not yours but God's. Tomorrow go down
against them. Behold, they will come up by the ascent of
Ziz. You will find them at the end of the valley, east of
the wilderness of Jeruel. You will not need to fight in this
battle. Stand firm, hold your position, and see the salvation of the Lord on your behalf, O Judah and Jerusalem.'
Do not be afraid and do not be dismayed. Tomorrow go
out against them, and the Lord will be with you."*

Lord, it is sometimes so hard to stand firm for you. I want to plot
and strategize, to scramble for solutions that aren't there. I look for
ways to attack, to defend myself and my reputation when enemies target me. Help me trust you, Mighty One. Help me rest in your presence
as you act on my behalf. Renew my confidence in you. Amen.

DAY 159

Romans 5:2-5

*Through him we have also obtained access by faith
into this grace in which we stand, and we rejoice in
hope of the glory of God. Not only that, but we rejoice
in our sufferings, knowing that suffering produces
endurance, and endurance produces character, and
character produces hope, and hope does not put us to
shame, because God's love has been poured into our hearts
through the Holy Spirit who has been given to us.*

Jailed in Indonesia for selling drugs, Mehfri came to faith in Christ by reading the book of Romans. After his release, Mehfri moved to a radical Muslim stronghold to share the gospel. "I saw God [was] with me completely," said Mehfri. (Read his full story on page 60.)

The Holy Spirit assures God's presence in your life as promised by Jesus Christ. As you lean on God, and your faith grows stronger, suffering can turn to good. You serve a God who can redeem anything!

DAY 160

2 Corinthians 5:5–7

He who has prepared us for this very thing is God, who has given us the Spirit as a guarantee. So we are always of good courage. We know that while we are at home in the body we are away from the Lord, for we walk by faith, not by sight.

To walk by faith means to trust God even when you cannot see him. Richard Wurmbrand endured solitary confinement for three years. He knew beyond all doubt he was not alone—that God was with him. To walk by faith means to face your life unafraid because you believe God's promise to be with you no matter what.

Comforted in Crisis

Eyewitnesses say the kidnapping of Malaysian pastor Raymond Koh unfolded like a scene from a movie. As Pastor Koh drove, three black SUVs surrounded his car and forced it to the side of the road. Men dressed in black scrambled out of their vehicles, grabbed Pastor Koh, and shoved him into one of the SUVs. The vehicles sped off in 40 seconds. No one has heard from him since.

Susanna, Pastor Koh's wife, is convinced his abduction is tied to a confrontation with the Selangor Islamic Department. Susanna and her husband had previously hosted a dinner for sponsors of a charity they founded to help the poor, single mothers, children, and others. Officers raided the event on the assumption that Pastor Koh shared the gospel with Muslims. He hadn't, but soon the intimidation began.

Death threats. Hate mail. A box containing two bullets—one each for Pastor Koh and his wife.

But even in the wake of the intimidation, Pastor Koh remained undeterred.

"He continued, though there was some fear and anxiety," says Susanna. "He felt that the Lord called him to fulfill the Great Commission, and that means [taking the gospel] to every tribe, nation, and tongue. So we just carried on our work with the poor, the needy, the marginalized, and with God's grace we carried through."

But then, the abduction happened.

Susanna went to the police, who were more intent on gathering information on Pastor Koh's activities than collecting details about the kidnapping.

Susanna knows her husband is in God's hands, but she misses him. "The hardest part is not knowing where he is, what happened to him, and how he is doing right now," she says.

God has used the Malaysian Christian community and the worldwide church to encourage Susanna and her three children. And God is comforting them.

"GOD HAS BEEN VERY REAL AND PERSONAL."

"God has been very real and personal to us," said Susanna. "I remember the first three weeks I was very lost and even had panic attacks. We decided to go for a silent retreat, and that helped me fix my eyes on Jesus. During that time, God spoke to me through his word."

One verse that became close to Susanna's heart is Psalm 46:10, which says, "Be still, and know that I am God."

"I don't need to struggle and strive," said Susanna. "I can just rest in the assurance that he is with me and he will never leave me or forsake me. He will work all things for good to those who love him and are called according to his purpose."

Susanna finds comfort in God's presence. As she trusts him, he gives her peace—and hope.

DAY 161

Isaiah 51:12

I, I am he who comforts you; who are you that you are afraid
of man who dies, of the son of man who is made like grass.

When living boldly for Christ, you may encounter the scorn of those around you. Their harassment or the humiliation they throw your way should not deter your faithfulness to God. After all, they are simply flesh and bone.

Don't fear man—man will die.

Richard Wurmbrand

WHOM SHALL I FEAR?

DAY 162

1 Chronicles 28:20

Then David said to Solomon his son, "Be strong and
courageous and do it. Do not be afraid and do not be
dismayed, for the LORD God, even my God, is with you.
He will not leave you or forsake you, until all the work
for the service of the house of the LORD is finished."

What might the Lord call you to do? Say it out loud and write it
below. Then take action on it.

_____

_____

_____

_____

_____

_____

DAY 163

Jeremiah 42:11

Do not fear the king of Babylon, of whom you are afraid.
Do not fear him, declares the LORD, for I am with
you, to save you and to deliver you from his hand.

Christians had a reason to fear the brutal Communist regime that imprisoned Richard Wurmbrand. But Richard understood that the King he served was mightier than any world government—that God's presence and protection were real. That was true then—and now. Since God is always with you, you don't have to fear rulers or regimes.

WHOM SHALL I FEAR?

DAY 164

2 Chronicles 32:7–8

"Be strong and courageous. Do not be afraid or dismayed
before the king of Assyria and all the horde that is with
him, for there are more with us than with him. With
him is an arm of flesh, but with us is the LORD our God,
to help us and to fight our battles." And the people took
confidence from the words of Hezekiah king of Judah.

Hezekiah encouraged his soldiers to not be afraid. Why? He knew
God would help them. Similarly outnumbered, Richard Wurmbrand stood for Christ at the Congress of Cults in Bucharest, Romania. One after another, bishops and pastors declared that Communism and Christianity were fundamentally the same. They assured the new government of their loyalty and chose Joseph Stalin—a mass murderer of Christians—as the honorary president of the congress. As God calls you to stand for him, realize that others may remain seated. And remember: when you stand with God, fear subsides as you trust him for help.

DAY 165

Jeremiah 46:27–28

"But fear not, O Jacob my servant, nor be dismayed, O Israel, for behold, I will save you from far away, and your offspring from the land of their captivity. Jacob shall return and have quiet and ease, and none shall make him afraid. Fear not, O Jacob my servant, declares the L*ORD, for I am with you. I will make a full end of all the nations to which I have driven you, but of you I will not make a full end. I will discipline you in just measure, and I will by no means leave you unpunished."*

Lord, you remove fear from my heart and heal the brokenness in me. Do your work in me, holy God. I accept your guidance and discipline as you restore me to wholeness, inside and out. Lead and I'll follow, Lord. Reveal my need for you, and I'll look at your truth, unafraid. Amen.

WHOM SHALL I FEAR?

DAY 166

Matthew 14:14–20

When he went ashore he saw a great crowd, and he had compassion on them and healed their sick. Now when it was evening, the disciples came to him and said, "This is a desolate place, and the day is now over; send the crowds away to go into the villages and buy food for themselves." But Jesus said, "They need not go away; you give them something to eat." They said to him, "We have only five loaves here and two fish." And he said, "Bring them here to me." Then he ordered the crowds to sit down on the grass, and taking the five loaves and the two fish, he looked up to heaven and said a blessing. Then he broke the loaves and gave them to the disciples, and the disciples gave them to the crowds. And they all ate and were satisfied. And they took up twelve baskets full of the broken pieces left over.

God lacks neither resources nor compassion. Tell him what you need. He's listening.

DAY 167

Psalm 34:17–19

*When the righteous cry for help, the LORD hears and
delivers them out of all their troubles. The LORD
is near to the brokenhearted and saves the crushed
in spirit. Many are the afflictions of the righteous,
but the LORD delivers him out of them all.*

Write down areas of your life that cause you to feel broken-hearted and crushed, and then tell a trusted friend. Together, ask God for deliverance.

DAY 168

Luke 21:17–19

You will be hated by all for my name's sake.
But not a hair of your head will perish. By
your endurance you will gain your lives.

People consumed by the things of this world despise biblical disciples. When you encounter hatred, even if it leads to physical death, endure it with joy. Why? Because your eternal life is just that: eternal. And as a biblical disciple, you live in the presence of God who provides for all your needs, because the Holy Spirit dwells in you.

DAY 169

1 Peter 5:10

And after you have suffered a little while, the God of all grace, who has called you to his eternal glory in Christ, will himself restore, confirm, strengthen, and establish you.

Faizah and her husband, Nagawo, left Islam to follow Christ. Then they served persecuted Christians in Ethiopia for the next thirty years. When Islamists beheaded Nagawo for his Christian witness and then set their home ablaze, Faizah experienced the presence of God. "He has helped me to pass through these difficulties, and I believe that he will help me even more," she said. VOM helped her rebuild her home, and she plans to continue sharing the gospel with Muslims.

Though you may suffer for a while, God will restore you. He will heal the bruised parts, and strengthen what is broken. God will provide for you, so fear not.

DAY 170

Psalm 139:1–3, 7–10

O LORD, you have searched me and known me! You know when I sit down and when I rise up; you discern my thoughts from afar. You search out my path and my lying down and are acquainted with all my ways. Where shall I go from your Spirit? Or where shall I flee from your presence? If I ascend to heaven, you are there! If I make my bed in Sheol, you are there! If I take the wings of the morning and dwell in the uttermost parts of the sea, even there your hand shall lead me, and your right hand shall hold me.

Lord, you know me through and through—I have no secrets from you. You know where fear finds me most vulnerable and when my thoughts spiral into dark places. Meet me there, Lord, and fight for me. I want to be free of what haunts me. I want to think first and foremost of you so that I can serve you faithfully. Amen.

Opposed, but Never Alone

For Fawzy, police interrogations come with the territory. As an evangelist and church planter in North Africa, Fawzy meets with new Christian converts and others interested in learning more about Jesus. The Islamic leaders and government officials view Fawzy's activities as a threat. The authorities fear civil unrest, so they frequently pull Fawzy into police stations for "meetings."

His first meeting occurred when Fawzy was seventeen, three months after he placed his faith in Christ. Arrested at home, he was interrogated for six hours about his decision to become a Christian. Although he was frightened, Fawzy's faith held strong.

"I felt like there was a power or a hope in my heart," said Fawzy, who boldly told police he'd left Islam for Christianity after studying the Bible through a correspondence course.

Three months later, the authorities again questioned Fawzy. He later learned the authorities hadn't arrested him because he was only seventeen years old. His release came with a warning: If he remained a Christian after his eighteenth birthday, he would spend the next two years in prison.

Much to Fawzy's relief, the authorities left him alone for the next fourteen years. His family, observant Muslims, also allowed him to practice his faith without harassment. Even his brother, a member of an extremist Muslim organization, told Fawzy he was the best of his brothers.

The police called him in for meetings again after Fawzy and another believer founded a church that grew to twenty members. Fawzy realized the police monitored his phone calls and watched him closely, but authorities were unable to charge him with anything, so he remained free.

After the government enacted an initiative to expel foreigners, some of whom were Christians, believers grew anxious, and attendance at Fawzy's house church dropped to only five people. As a church planter, Fawzy became even more visible to authorities. The frequency of police interrogations picked up, but Fawzy remained unafraid of those encounters.

> "EVEN WHEN THE AUTHORITIES ARE AGAINST YOU, GOD IS WITH YOU."

Perhaps Fawzy's trustworthy reputation, which extends even to the security forces, helps. "They sit with me in the coffee shop," Fawzy says. "They…know everything, every detail. [They say,] 'We know that you are a Christian for more than twenty years. We know that you attend church. We know you are a true believer in Christ. But at the same time, [we] understand that you have a good relationship and you behave in a good way with respect toward people.'"

Fawzy tells the security officers his honesty is a result of his faith in Christ.

Another reason Fawzy is unafraid of his encounters with authorities: He considers every interrogation an opportunity to boldly share his faith. When Fawzy walks into a police station, he walks in accompanied by someone else; God is present with Fawzy wherever he goes.

"Even when the authorities are against you, God is with you," Fawzy said. "My main concern is how I can testify to God's work."

DAY 171

Acts 13:44–46, 48, 52

*The next Sabbath almost the whole city gathered to hear
the word of the Lord. But when the Jews saw the crowds,
they were filled with jealousy and began to contradict what
was spoken by Paul, reviling him. And Paul and Barnabas
spoke out boldly, saying, "It was necessary that the word of
God be spoken first to you. Since you thrust it aside and
judge yourselves unworthy of eternal life, behold, we are
turning to the Gentiles." And when the Gentiles heard this,
they began rejoicing and glorifying the word of the Lord,
and as many as were appointed to eternal life believed. And
the disciples were filled with joy and with the Holy Spirit.*

The opposition was stiff, the criticism biting. Yet Paul and Barnabas spoke words of life, and transformation occurred in those who were willing to hear. Fear did not muzzle Paul and Barnabas—don't let fear muzzle you. Boldly speak out the gospel. Boldly live out your calling. Praise and glorify your God with all you say and do!

DAY 172

Joshua 1:9

*[The Lord said to Joshua], "Have I not com-
manded you? Be strong and courageous. Do not
be frightened, and do not be dismayed, for the
Lord your God is with you wherever you go."*

Nothing invites confusion and dismay into our lives quicker than
fear. And nothing tames those twin beasts faster than trusting
our ever-present God. When eighteen-year-old Boupha faced interrogation by Laotian Communist officials for her Christian work, she felt
afraid. But then she prayed, "Lord, please help me," and she boldly
shared the gospel with her interrogators.

Like Boupha, you can rely on God—he is with you wherever you
go. Take time right now to thank him that his enduring presence will
be with you every second of the day.

DAY 173

Philippians 4:11-13, 19

Not that I am speaking of being in need, for I have learned in whatever situation I am to be content. I know how to be brought low, and I know how to abound. In any and every circumstance, I have learned the secret of facing plenty and hunger, abundance and need. I can do all things through him who strengthens me. And my God will supply every need of yours according to his riches in glory in Christ Jesus.

Lord, you are the giver of all that's good and true. You satisfy my spirit and attend to my needs. I trust you to supply what's needed from the great abundance of your riches and glory. I come before you in obedience to Christ. Amen.

DAY 174

Isaiah 43:1–2

But now thus says the Lord, *he who created you, O Jacob, he who formed you, O Israel: "Fear not, for I have redeemed you; I have called you by name, you are mine. When you pass through the waters, I will be with you; and through the rivers, they shall not overwhelm you; when you walk through fire you shall not be burned, and the flame shall not consume you."*

When you belong to the Lord, he is present even as floodwaters rise and wildfires rush toward you. Yes, you may suffer pain— but only for the moment. You are not alone in facing trouble. God is present—now and always!

DAY 175

2 Timothy 1:7

*For God gave us a spirit not of fear but of
power and love and self-control.*

When Hindu radicals killed Huldah's husband, a pastor in India, Huldah feared they might come for her, too. She prayed,
"Lord, give me boldness because your word has said that you have not
given the spirit of fear." Let her prayer be the posture of your heart today as you live in obedience to Christ.

DAY 176

Psalm 16:1–2, 8–9

*Preserve me, O God, for in you I take refuge. I say to the
Lord, "You are my Lord; I have no good apart from you."
I have set the Lord always before me; because he is at my
right hand, I shall not be shaken. Therefore my heart is glad,
and my whole being rejoices; my flesh also dwells secure.*

Your presence gladdens my heart, Lord. You displayed your love
for me in the cross of Christ, and every ounce of me delights in
you. In you, I am safe, secure, and unshakable from any circumstance
or even any person who may oppose my witness for you. May I choose
to walk in the reality of your presence. Amen.

DAY 177

2 Corinthians 9:8–10

And God is able to make all grace abound to you, so that
having all sufficiency in all things at all times, you may
abound in every good work. As it is written, "He has
distributed freely, he has given to the poor; his righteous-
ness endures forever." He who supplies seed to the sower
and bread for food will supply and multiply your seed for
sowing and increase the harvest of your righteousness.

What seeds do you sow? Seeds of fear and anxiety or seeds of faith? The thoughts you plant in your heart and mind will grow there. Ask the God who loves you to draw you ever closer to him, and in obedience choose to trust him. He provides all you need to live a joyful life—plant seeds of faith deeply in your heart and mind.

DAY 178

Exodus 33:14–15

And he [the Lord] said, "My presence will go with you, and I will give you rest." And he [Moses] said to him, "If your presence will not go with me, do not bring us up from here."

When persecuted Christians endure the harshest, coldest of prison cells, his presence can help them rest. In the Soviet Union, Nadejda Sloboda came to Christ through a Russian gospel broadcast. She immediately shared the gospel in her village and formed a church, drawing the attention of Communist authorities who sentenced her to four years in prison. But even in prison, Nadejda continued to share the gospel and was soon punished with two months in an unheated, isolated cell where she slept on concrete with no mattress. How was it possible for her to rest? "I fall asleep on the cold concrete floor trusting in God, and it becomes warm around me," she said. "I rest in the arms of God."

How does Nadejda's story inspire you today?

God's Protection:
Our Shield and Refuge

When you first heard about Jesus, someone probably told you that Jesus loves you, that he came to save you, and that heaven is in your future. And that between now and then, you can experience purpose and joy.

And that's true, all of it.

But did anyone mention that following Jesus Christ often steers people straight into danger? That living kingdom values in a fallen world will attract opposition from those trying to silence your witness?

Jesus warned his first disciples that following him would be costly. Friends, family, homes—all could be lost. They could expect to be mocked, beaten, even martyred. Obeying Christ meant putting him first, always.

Many people—including, perhaps, you—expect the life of a Christian to result in a life free from harm, difficulty, and suffering. And nothing could be further from the truth.

Yes, sometimes God intervenes with supernatural protection to preserve the life and witness of Christians boldly living out their faith. It happens, but there's no guarantee.

Still, remaining in step with God's will as biblical disciples and grasping that God ultimately knows the number of your days bring such relief. Such confidence comes with the assurance God is in control and holds you close in his mighty arms!

GOD'S PROTECTION IS MORE LIKE A SHIELD IN BATTLE THAN A SECURITY BLANKET FOR OUR COMFORT AT HOME.

Sabina Wurmbrand often told the story of Lidia. Imprisoned for her faith in a Siberian labor camp in the Soviet Union, Lidia worked hard to meet her daily quota. But when the thieves and robbers imprisoned with her stole the work she had completed for the day, Lidia went without dinner.

Hungry and unable to sleep, Lidia left her cell and walked out into the prison yard.

Lidia began to pray and weep, and then she heard a man's voice call after her. She looked behind her and saw a Soviet officer with a revolver in his hand. "Hey, do you have a mother who prays for you?" he asked.

"Oh, yes," she replied.

"For half an hour, I have been running after you with this revolver to shoot you because you are where you are not allowed to be," he told her. "But now I cannot move my arm. It is surely your mother who prays for you. Now run back immediately, because if someone sees us here, he will shoot us both."

Lidia ran back to her prison cell, weeping tears of gratitude. She slept as if she had eaten the best of dinners. In the morning, the Soviet guard showed Lidia his arm. He was now able to move it.

Among the thousands of forgotten prisoners, God took care of his child, Lidia. He even showed the Communist guard that a mother who prays can help her child—even if the child was in a Communist prison.

We like to play it safe. We like security over adventure. We prefer comfort to challenge. We want to safeguard our lives from as much doubt and fear as possible. Yet, we forget that God offers his protection at times when we are on the frontlines in his service. God's protection is more like a shield in battle than a security blanket for our comfort at home.

Fear becomes a temporary spike in your blood pressure rather than a force that controls you. God will help shift your perspective from the immediate to the eternal. God makes his peace available to people who know to whom they belong.

DAY 179

Genesis 15:1

After these things the word of the LORD came to Abram in a vision: "Fear not, Abram, I am your shield; your reward shall be very great."

Citizens in many nations experience a measure of protection from their own government. Christians in restricted nations, however, don't receive protection from their governments. Yet, the church grows in these countries as more and more people hear the gospel through the bold witness of Christ's followers. These Christians daily count the cost of boldly following Jesus and trusting him to be their shield—until his work on earth for them is accomplished, and they enter their reward.

How does this example from persecuted Christians inspire you today?

DAY 180

Nahum 1:7

The Lord is good, a stronghold in the day of trouble; he knows those who take refuge in him.

In Old Testament times, a stronghold referred to a place of refuge from attack, often a cave or cliff or other inaccessible place to an enemy. How are you taking refuge in the Lord today?

> Under the shadow of your throne
> your saints have dwelt secure;
> sufficient is your arm alone,
> and our defense is sure.
>> "O God, Our Help in Ages Past," hymn by Isaac Watts

WHOM SHALL I FEAR?

DAY 181

Psalm 10:17–18

O LORD, you hear the desire of the afflicted; you will strengthen their heart; you will incline your ear to do justice to the fatherless and the oppressed, so that man who is of the earth may strike terror no more.

A young Pakistani girl, Anila, lives with her older sister, mother, and alcoholic father. Since her father spends the family's money on his addiction, Anila has to carry her books to school in a sack. Through her neighbor's influence, Anila attends Sunday school and is eager to memorize Bible verses. She prays that Jesus will change her dad's heart. Recently, Anila was overjoyed to receive a backpack and a children's Bible from local Christians. After receiving these gifts, she believes God, through his grace, will change her father, and the joy of their family will be restored.

How are you encouraging others today despite anxiety you may feel?

DAY 182

Isaiah 54:16–17

Behold, I have created the smith who blows the fire of coals and produces a weapon for its purpose. I have also created the ravager to destroy; no weapon that is fashioned against you shall succeed, and you shall refute every tongue that rises against you in judgment. This is the heritage of the servants of the LORD and their vindication from me, declares the LORD.

Those who persecute our brothers and sisters in Christ wield fear as a weapon—fear of arrest, torture, pain, and shame. Yet God promises no weapon fashioned against his children will succeed. God empowers each of us to stand in the face of our fear as he uses us to advance his kingdom.

> For we are firmly convinced that we can suffer no evil unless we are proved to be evildoers or shown to be criminals. You can kill us, but cannot do us any real harm.
>
> Justin Martyr in his First Apology, an address to the emperor of Rome in the second century

DAY 183

Proverbs 29:25

The fear of man lays a snare, but who-
*ever trusts in the L*ORD *is safe.*

As Roberto looked back on his life, he felt like he hadn't amounted to much. He felt empty, and his heart was full of hate. As a member of a rebel group in Southern Mexico, his work involved stealing money, running drugs, and fighting the government. His life lacked meaning, and now he felt trapped by the rebel "cause." Roberto decided he would go elsewhere and try to make money. But the trip didn't go well; Roberto fell from the train and severed his left arm. The fall left him with multiple fractures. As he lay on the ground in pain, he recalled the words of a street preacher he'd once heard in a park, and his thoughts turned to God. "Give me life, and I'll get up, and I'll look for you and I'll speak about you," he prayed.

God answered Roberto's prayers. He survived the accident, returned to his home, and became an itinerant preacher.

DAY 184

Genesis 50:20–21

[Joseph said to his brothers]: "As for you, you meant evil
against me, but God meant it for good, to bring it about
that many people should be kept alive, as they are today.
So do not fear; I will provide for you and your little ones."
Thus he comforted them and spoke kindly to them.

After the Allied powers defeated the Nazis in World War II, the
hunter became the hunted. Russian Communist troops poured
into Romania in August of 1944. Left behind in the retreat, German
soldiers had to fend for themselves, and many died. While Richard and
Sabina Wurmbrand were utterly opposed to the Nazis, they could not
refuse to help the Germans. Many of the remaining soldiers were starv-
ing and terrified. People told the Wurmbrands, "You're taking foolish
risks for the sake of murderers." But Richard answered, "God is always
on the side of the persecuted."

How does the Wurmbrands' example challenge and inspire you?

DAY 185

Psalm 138:7

*Though I walk in the midst of trouble, you preserve
my life; you stretch out your hand against the wrath
of my enemies, and your right hand delivers me.*

Trouble can roll in from all sides—sometimes because of what we've done or left undone, sometimes for no cause at all. Remember: God is in the rescue business. Trust in him—he will safely usher you into his eternal kingdom.

DAY 186

Isaiah 41:13–14

For I, the LORD your God, hold your right hand;
it is I who say to you, "Fear not, I am the one who
helps you." Fear not, you worm Jacob, you men
of Israel! I am the one who helps you, declares the
LORD; your Redeemer is the Holy One of Israel.

Jacob swindled his brother, Esau, out of his birthright. Then Jacob deceived his father, Isaac, so that he also received the blessing that his father had intended for Esau. Separated from his family, Jacob lived in fear of his brother's revenge. When God told Jacob to return to his father's land, he worried about the brother he had wronged. How would Esau receive him? But God promised protection, and in obedience, Jacob humbly walked home. Esau forgave Jacob, and Jacob lived a transformed life.

What is God calling you to do in obedience? Do you trust God enough to do what he is calling you to do? Set aside your fear and walk in obedience.

DAY 187

Psalm 64:9–10

*Then all mankind fears; they tell what God has
brought about and ponder what he has done. Let
the righteous one rejoice in the Lord and take refuge in him! Let all the upright in heart exult!*

The apostle Paul wrote about rejoicing. "Rejoice in the Lord always, and again I say rejoice!" (Philippians 4:4). He wrote those
words while chained in a Roman prison. It's counterintuitive to declare that a person should rejoice when his future is uncertain. But the
apostle left us an example to rejoice in the Lord as we take refuge in
him, regardless of our circumstances.

Do a little pondering today. What has God done in your life? Write
it down in the space below and celebrate it today.

Taking Jesus into the Jungle

David and Gloria Martinez moved deep into one of Colombia's "red zones," areas controlled by violent Marxist guerrilla and paramilitary groups. The couple wanted to share the gospel, distribute Bibles, and plant churches. They studied the local language and learned to live off the land while they built relationships among the region's indigenous people. David and Gloria grew accustomed to living near right-wing paramilitary groups and armed rebel groups, such as the National Liberation Army (ELN) and Revolutionary Armed Forces of Colombia (FARC).

Slowly they began to train church leaders and establish churches. As a result, many people came to faith in Christ. "That is when it got difficult," Gloria says. "The devil was mad. The spiritual attacks started. The witchcraft and the different armed groups started to come in."

The couple, who had a nine-month-old daughter, begged God for protection.

A year after David and Gloria moved to the red zone, a prominent guerrilla commander in Colombia declared all pastors in the area objects of war. About the same time, David and Gloria caught the attention of locals who hauled cocaine to boats along the coast. "People would say, 'Hey, these foreigners are seeing what we're doing,'" David recalls. "We had to decide if we were going to leave or stay. Our decision was to stay because we were preaching the gospel."

Then, one day a rebel leader accompanied by about sixty guerrilla soldiers came to the couple's house and told David he had to support the guerrillas. "They knew everything about me," he said. "They mentioned all my wife's family members, [and] all of my family members. They knew the offering I was receiving every three months. They knew the exact amount we were receiving."

One of the rebels told David that they would triple his salary and allow him to continue his pastoral work if David would join them, as other pastors already had. "If they are collaborating, they are no longer pastors," David replied. "I won't work with you. You kill people. The only person who should have power over life is God."

"OUR DECISION WAS TO STAY."

The rebel leader didn't appreciate David's boldness. "You are lucky it's me and not some other guerrillas, as they would have shot you in the head already," he said. "We are going to talk tomorrow."

Holding their daughter, Samantha, Gloria began to pray for the protection of her husband and daughter. "A lot of the guerrillas are famous for taking kids," she said. "I feared for both of them."

The next day, the rebel leader and sixty guerrillas returned to David and Gloria's house, but this time, the leader had a changed attitude. He told David that his mother was a Christian. Surprised and relieved, David relaxed as the two began to discuss the Bible. "When we started to speak about God, I started to become his friend," David said. "I became good friends with this man. I told him to listen to God. He said, 'I will only come to Christ when I am injured in the war.'"

David urged the man to place his faith in Jesus as Savior before he died in the conflict, but the man resisted. Before the rebel leader left, he accepted sixty Bibles from David to share with the other fighters.

Fifteen days later, a paramilitary group attacked and killed the rebel leader.

The rebel groups continued to control every aspect of David and Gloria's lives. To buy food and other goods, they had to walk through both FARC and paramilitary territories. "Every time we passed the paramilitary, they thought we were collaborators with the guerrillas," said David. "They threatened us. They told the indigenous people they were going to kill us."

When community members relayed the threats to David and Gloria, the couple decided to transfer to a safer part of the province. With local pastors in place, David and Gloria left the area confident the believers would be well cared for.

Despite their difficulties, David and Gloria left in awe of all that God had done in one of Colombia's red zones. In five years, they saw him raise up four indigenous pastors, and they planted churches in two communities.

In those two communities, seventy people came to faith in Jesus Christ.

DAY 188

John 7:43–44

So there was a division among the people over him. Some of them wanted to arrest him, but no one laid hands on him.

Sooner or later, it's a decision everyone faces: *What will I do with Jesus?* Write your answer below.

_____

_____

_____

_____

_____

_____

_____

DAY 189

Jeremiah 15:20–21

And I will make you to this people a fortified wall of bronze; they will fight against you, but they shall not prevail over you, for I am with you to save you and deliver you, declares the LORD. I will deliver you out of the hand of the wicked, and redeem you from the grasp of the ruthless.

It sometimes seems that God's protection isn't visible to our human eyes. In restricted nations and hostile areas, pastors are jailed, Christians are martyred, and believers are oppressed by governments without any apparent consequences. But in the end, evil won't prevail. God will be victorious. You will be redeemed from this broken world by your mighty God. A day is coming when justice will shine, and God will reign on earth as he reigns in heaven. His protection and provision are real!

DAY 190

Psalm 3:5–6

I lay down and slept; I woke again, for the LORD sustained me. I will not be afraid of many thousands of people who have set themselves against me all around.

I magine being able to sleep peacefully despite thousands of people rising up against you, closing in to kill you. Sleep in such a situation seems unthinkable—unless you have security in the Lord.

I praise you, God, for sustaining your people who serve with courage!

DAY 191

2 Samuel 22:47–49

The LORD lives, and blessed be my rock, and exalted be
my God, the rock of my salvation, the God who gave me
vengeance and brought down peoples under me, who
brought me out from my enemies; you exalted me above those
who rose against me; you delivered me from men of violence.

When Surita left Buddhism to follow Christ, her father-in-law became enraged. His verbal attacks led to physical attacks, and he grabbed Surita's Bible and beat her with it. Surita later reflected, "At the time, I was remembering the pain of Christ on the cross. I thought if Christ suffered for me and gave his life for me, then this is a privilege for me to suffer for Him." Surita's perspective gave her victory over the evil intent of her persecutor.

Lord, you anchor your people. You are our firm foundation, the rock of our salvation, the God who wins battles when we are far too weak to fight. You are our Deliverer, Holy One. You are our God now and forever. Amen.

WHOM SHALL I FEAR?

DAY 192

Acts 12:6

*Now when Herod was about to bring him out,
on that very night, Peter was sleeping between
two soldiers, bound with two chains, and sentries
before the door were guarding the prison.*

P eter was trapped by chains and a prison door, but he wasn't worried. He was right where God wanted him so that God could fulfill his purposes through Peter. Don't let circumstances impact your faith in your Father; he's far bigger than your circumstances. Better to be in prison with him than unchained without him.

DAY 193

Psalm 91:1–6

He who dwells in the shelter of the Most High will abide in the shadow of the Almighty. I will say to the LORD, "My refuge and my fortress, my God, in whom I trust." For he will deliver you from the snare of the fowler and from the deadly pestilence. He will cover you with his pinions, and under his wings you will find refuge; his faithfulness is a shield and buckler. You will not fear the terror of the night, nor the arrow that flies by day, nor the pestilence that stalks in darkness, nor the destruction that wastes at noonday.

Young children find great comfort by sticking close to adults they trust. Parents, grandparents, and others cast a shadow of protection, like the protection we find when we're near God. As we walk in obedience, that shadow travels with us, protecting us from any snare or terror.

WHOM SHALL I FEAR?

DAY 194

Exodus 14:13–14

*And Moses said to the people, "Fear not, stand firm,
and see the salvation of the Lord, which he will
work for you today. For the Egyptians whom you
see today, you shall never see again. The Lord will
fight for you, and you have only to be silent."*

Silently consider: Where do you see God's salvation in your life?
Where is God fighting for you? How are you standing firm instead
of retreating when fear rises up in your mind?

DAY 195

Psalm 121:1–3

I lift up my eyes to the hills. From where does my help come? My help comes from the LORD, who made heaven and earth. He will not let your foot be moved; he who keeps you will not slumber.

Who do you call first when troubles flood in? Call out to God—his help will keep you from being swept away.

WHOM SHALL I FEAR?

Fourteen Christmases in Prison
By Richard Wurmbrand

It was Christmas Eve, and Richard Wurmbrand had just returned to his cell after twelve hours of slave labor in the bitter Romanian winter. His body ached, he was shivering, and his stomach churned with hunger.

For another hour, Captain Stan kept Richard and his fellow prisoners standing at attention. "I can crack any of you with one punch," he shouted. "I promise that for tomorrow's feast you'll be beaten worse than ever. Christ was not born for you. Nobody loves you. Your wives are now with other men. Your children are now Communists and curse you. Merry Christmas."

After the captain left, one of Richard's cellmates, Pastor Craciun, stretched out his weakened body on the few wooden planks that served as a bed. He whispered to Richard, "Tomorrow might be unpleasant, but 'he who keeps Israel will neither slumber nor sleep'" (Psalm 121:4).

A moment later, in spite of the cold and hunger, Pastor Craciun was sleeping peacefully. But during the fourteen Christmases Richard spent in prison, he met some who couldn't sleep as peacefully as Pastor Craciun.

One such man was Sepeanu, a former colonel in the Communist secret police. As he lay dying in Richard's cell he cried, "Help me! I have tortured many innocents. I am going to hell!"

Another pastor in the cell spoke up. "No sin against God's majesty goes without punishment, but Jesus has borne the punishment due to us. Through his blood we are saved from hell."

The Communist torturer was converted, meeting Jesus that day.

Another Christmas Eve, an abbot named Iscu lay in a bed on Richard's right, awaiting death from the tortures he'd endured. The abbot was serene, knowing he'd soon be with Jesus in heaven.

On Richard's left was another prisoner—the man who had tortured Iscu. His comrades had turned on him, and he, too, had been imprisoned and tortured.

"PASTOR CRACIUN WAS SLEEPING PEACEFULLY."

Distraught, this torturer woke Richard during the night. "I have committed horrible crimes," he confessed. "I can find no rest. Help me."

Just then, Iscu called two other prisoners to his side to help him. Leaning on them, he walked slowly to his former torturer and sat down at his bedside.

"You were young and did not know what you were doing," Iscu said, caressing the man's head. "I forgive and love you, as do all the other Christians you mistreated. And if we sinners who have been saved by Jesus can love like this, how much more is he ready to erase all the evil you have done, to cleanse you fully. Only repent."

In that common cell in which there was no privacy, Richard heard the torturer confessing his crimes to the tortured. And he overheard the tortured absolving his torturer before they embraced.

Both men died that night, on Christmas Eve.

"This is the real meaning of Christmas," Richard wrote. "Such men love the cross and endure its humiliation. They follow the Man of Sorrows in suffering that has been freely chosen for the sake of truth."

DAY 196

Isaiah 52:12

*For you shall not go out in haste, and you shall
not go in flight, for the LORD will go before you,
and the God of Israel will be your rear guard.*

When troops move through hostile territory, they are most vulnerable from the front and the rear. You also travel through dangerous terrain, constantly tempted and under attack by Satan as you move in obedience on Christ's behalf. Thank God for his protection!

DAY 197

Jeremiah 17:17

*Be not a terror to me; you are my
refuge in the day of disaster.*

Disasters are a reality of life in a fallen world. Neither natural disasters nor manmade disasters are in short supply. But don't be distracted by the "what ifs" of disasters. Instead, trust in the God who's always able to put the pieces back together—for his glory and the advancement of his kingdom.

DAY 198

2 Timothy 4:18

At my first defense no one came to stand by me, but all deserted me. May it not be charged against them! But the Lord stood by me and strengthened me, so that through me the message might be fully proclaimed and all the Gentiles might hear it. So I was rescued from the lion's mouth. The Lord will rescue me from every evil deed and bring me safely into his heavenly kingdom. To him be the glory forever and ever. Amen.

Persecuted Christians in regions hostile to the gospel are constantly at risk of being betrayed by people they know and love. In many places, governments urge their citizens to inform on people—even on their family's Christian activities. When a believer is betrayed and the betrayal ends in death, God promises to usher them safely into his heavenly kingdom.

DAY 199

Psalm 32:7

You are a hiding place for me; you preserve me from
trouble; you surround me with shouts of deliverance.

Hiding places aren't permanent—they're temporary shelters where you can find renewal from feelings of discouragement, anxiety, or helplessness. In those places, God surrounds you with encouragement so you can engage again fully with his mission. Where are you today—in a hiding place, in need of one, or walking in bold obedience?

DAY 200

1 John 5:18

*We know that everyone who has been born of God
does not keep on sinning, but he who was born of God
protects him, and the evil one does not touch him.*

Read this passage out loud. Taste the words. Hear their promise.
And fear not—you are protected from the evil one!

DAY 201

Psalm 3:3

But You, O Lord, are a shield about me,
my glory, and the lifter of my head.

Lord, when I'm drifting toward despair about myself or my situation, I remember your love shields me. Your grace infuses me with life. Thank you for caring for me, Lord. Thank you for gently lifting my chin so my eyes can look past my fears and focus on you. Amen.

DAY 202

Isaiah 41:8–10

But you, Israel, my servant, Jacob, whom I have chosen, the offspring of Abraham, my friend; you whom I took from the ends of the earth, and called from its farthest corners, saying to you, "You are my servant, I have chosen you and not cast you off"; fear not, for I am with you; be not dismayed, for I am your God; I will strengthen you, I will help you, I will uphold you with my righteous right hand.

One fear can often haunt us, one we're sometimes ashamed to admit: the fear of rejection. We want to be accepted, invited, included. When that doesn't happen, the pain can be intense. Here's a truth for you: God will never reject you. In Christ, he has chosen you to be his, and he claims you as his own. You are secure in his everlasting love.

DAY 203

Psalm 59:16

But I will sing of your strength; I will sing aloud of your steadfast love in the morning. For you have been to me a fortress and a refuge in the day of my distress.

In the Philippines, Ruth was frightened one night by the sound of nearby fighting. She ran with her husband, Armando, and their children behind their house and searched for a place to hide. They saw nothing better than a small footbridge that crossed a murky canal behind their house. They quickly crawled under it. They knew there were snakes in the water, but they chose the danger of the snakes over that of the Muslim rebels they could hear advancing toward their village. The couple tried to quiet their girls, but they were scared and crying. "We were praying to the Lord to cover us with his precious blood, asking for him to protect us," Ruth said. They passed the next eight hours until daylight by praying, quietly singing, and talking.

Sing a song praising God for his protection.

DAY 204

Joel 3:16

*The LORD roars from Zion, and utters his voice
from Jerusalem, and the heavens and the earth
quake. But the LORD is a refuge to his people,
a stronghold to the people of Israel.*

Lord, even the echo of your voice sends stars scattering. A mere
trace of your holiness causes the cosmos to fall to its knees in worship. You are mighty beyond measure yet gentle with those who love
you. Thank you for your love, Father. Thank you for being my refuge
and stronghold when danger comes. Amen.

WHOM SHALL I FEAR?

Psalm 18:30

This God—his way is perfect; the word of the LORD proves true; he is a shield for all those who take refuge in him.

L ord, what a place of refuge you provide! You know my heart and see my wounds. You bring healing to the pain I reveal and the pain I hide. Your power is absolute, Lord, and your mercy everlasting. I give myself to you, battered as I am, and ask for you to shield me from all that would draw me away from you. In you is life, Lord. Amen.

DAY 206

John 17:15–16

*"I do not ask that you take them out of the world,
but that you keep them from the evil one. They are
not of the world, just as I am not of the world."*

In Christ's prayer, he asks his Father to keep his followers "from the evil one." Think about that. And as you do, remember that this world is just temporary because this world isn't your home. One day, you'll move on, and what you fear won't travel with you. God will rescue you, and you'll leave your fear behind.

God's Assignment:
Living on Purpose

Fourteen years. Fourteen long, painful years.

That's 5,110 mornings Richard Wurmbrand opened his eyes to confront the cement walls of a prison cell and the following question: *What's my purpose?*

Before Richard's arrest, the answer was simple. He was a pastor, teacher, husband, and father. Any of those answers could fill a lifetime. But here in this cell—for years in solitary confinement—why was life worth living? What could he contribute? *What was his purpose?*

Richard knew the answer because he was a disciple before he was anything else. Richard had committed his life to following Jesus Christ and joining his redemptive plan for humanity. If Richard could, he'd witness to the truth of the gospel. If no one else was present, he'd pray for the kingdom of God to advance beyond and within the walls of his prison.

Richard was on an assignment given to him by the Lord Jesus Christ—and there's no greater purpose than that. He wrote:

> Fear is…a decisive hindrance to Christian life in the free world. We fear we will have to suffer in our family, in our jobs or in our finances if we obey a commandment of Christ. We also fear mistakes in life, but the greatest mistake is to fear mistakes.
>
> God's Word has to be spread, despite mistakes in Christian work. Tragedies might ensue, but they only underscore the importance of spreading the Word of God. We all have tasks from God. It is better to fulfill them with mistakes than to leave them unfulfilled. Do not fear. Our models are Christians who have conquered fear.

It's likely you didn't wake up in a prison cell this morning. But wherever you opened your eyes, you opened them to the same assignment given to Richard.

Christ calls you to love God with all your heart, mind, and strength; to love others as you love yourself. And to share his love through word and deed with everyone who enters your sphere of influence and all who are open to hearing the gospel.

Don't let opposition stop you or circumstances distract you. Don't let fear sideline you.

You have a purpose, and an assignment.

And you haven't yet finished.

DAY 207

Matthew 28:19–20

"Go therefore and make disciples of all nations,
baptizing them in the name of the Father and of
the Son and of the Holy Spirit, teaching them to
observe all that I have commanded you. And behold,
I am with you always, to the end of the age."

Vee, a widow in her seventies who lives in Communist Laos, suffered from long-term health problems. When traditional healers
who prayed to ancestors and other remedies didn't work, she turned
to Christians for prayer. And she was healed! Soon, Vee committed
her life to Christ and shared her new faith with everyone she met. Vee
even walked two hours to another village to share the gospel. Village
authorities tried to stop her and Sun, another woman Vee had led to
Christ. Sun said about the persecution they encountered, "It was like
the Lord was really with me at that moment."

Vee said, "It made me stronger."

How does their testimony inspire you to share your faith with
someone today?

DAY 208

2 Timothy 4:5–8

As for you, always be sober-minded, endure suffering, do the work of an evangelist, fulfill your ministry. For I am already being poured out as a drink offering, and the time of my departure has come. I have fought the good fight, I have finished the race, I have kept the faith. Henceforth there is laid up for me the crown of righteousness, which the Lord, the righteous judge, will award to me on that day, and not only to me but also to all who have loved his appearing.

World-class runners focus like a laser on the finish. Knowing what awaits them at the end of their striving gives the runners courage to persevere through tension, fear, and temporary pain. What temporary pain are you overcoming to run with endurance? Focus on your finish. Think about the glorious gift God has waiting for you when you faithfully complete your course.

DAY 209

Acts 1:8

"But you will receive power when the Holy Spirit has come upon you, and you will be my witnesses in Jerusalem and in all Judea and Samaria, and to the end of the earth."

Thank you, Lord, for giving me a purpose and providing the power of the Holy Spirit to propel me to boldness. When I'm weak, the strength of the Holy Spirit is strong. When I'm afraid, the indwelling presence of your Holy Spirit is more than enough to enable me to complete the work you've put before me. I pray that you give me an opportunity to be your witness to someone today. I praise you, Lord. Amen.

DAY 210

Deuteronomy 1:21

See, the LORD your God has set the land before you.
Go up, take possession, as the LORD, the God of your
fathers, has told you. Do not fear or be dismayed.

John is a front-line worker in Myanmar who trains Christian missionaries to share the gospel on some of the country's most hostile mission fields. Often called to the police station to face interrogation, John combats fear by realizing the assignment God gave him is greater than any other pursuit in his life. John once boldly told the police, "You do what you must do, and I will do what I must do." What mission field has the Lord revealed to you to take possession of today?

DAY 211

Acts 27:14–15, 18–19, 22–24

*But soon a tempestuous wind, called the northeaster,
struck down from the land. And when the ship was caught
and could not face the wind, we gave way to it and were
driven along. Since we were violently storm-tossed, they
began the next day to jettison the cargo. And on the third
day they threw the ship's tackle overboard with their own
hands. Yet now I urge you to take heart, for there will be
no loss of life among you, but only of the ship. For this
very night there stood before me an angel of the God to
whom I belong and whom I worship, and he said, "Do
not be afraid, Paul; you must stand before Caesar."*

Not every storm that runs you aground may be from God, but
God uses every tempest you encounter to help you trust him.
And when your faith grows stronger than your fear, you can live boldly.
What tempests are you facing right now? How can you live in bold
obedience even amid those storms?

DAY 212

2 Timothy 2:10

*Therefore I endure everything for the sake of
the elect, that they also may obtain the salvation that is in Christ Jesus with eternal glory.*

Lord, please give me the courage, strength, and endurance to fulfill
my part of your magnificent purpose. Where there's hardship, let
me faithfully prevail. Where there's opposition, let me courageously
remain faithful and obedient. Where there's little, let me be content
knowing that a little in your hands is more than enough. I pray this for
myself and each of my brothers and sisters in Christ around the world.
Amen.

DAY 213

Psalm 138:7–8

Though I walk in the midst of trouble, you preserve my life; you stretch out your hand against the wrath of my enemies, and your right hand delivers me. The LORD will fulfill his purpose for me; your steadfast love, O LORD, endures forever. Do not forsake the work of your hands.

Lord, I'm thankful that in hard times, you're my comfort. Even when my enemies seem strong, you're stronger. When I share your story, you are with me. Please protect and encourage all whose lives are endangered by their witness for you. Walk with them, Lord. Amen.

DAY 214

Luke 10:1–3

*After this the Lord appointed seventy-two others and
sent them on ahead of him, two by two, into every town
and place where he himself was about to go. And he said
to them, "The harvest is plentiful, but the laborers are
few. Therefore pray earnestly to the Lord of the harvest to
send out laborers into his harvest. Go your way; behold,
I am sending you out as lambs in the midst of wolves."*

At nine a.m., the beatings started. Police officers dragged the two
bruised Vietnamese evangelists Hy and Tan out of the police station and into the village square. A large crowd gathered to beat these
"propagators of lies and rebellion." As more than one hundred people
stepped forward to strike the evangelists, the two men remained silent.
"Dog men!" jeered the watching crowd. The beating lasted for three
hours.

Like the seventy-two sent out as lambs among wolves, Hy and Tan
fulfilled their assignment. What assignment is God calling you to fulfill
today? What price might you prepare to pay?

Matthew 20:28

"Even as the Son of Man came not to be served but to serve, and to give his life as a ransom for many."

The morning after Sudanese Air Force bombers struck his village in Sudan's Nuba Mountains, Pastor Morris prepared to go to jail. The pastor had done nothing wrong. He went by choice, in obedience to Christ's command to "Love your enemies." For Pastor Morris, that meant packing soap, food, clothes, and shoes to give to Muslim prisoners of war who served the same government that had bombed his village the previous night. The visits have borne fruit. Hearts have changed. Even in jail, the prisoners found freedom.

As Christ's disciples, we're called to live in service to others. What's one way you can honor Jesus today by serving someone in his name?

A Father's Legacy

Emmanuel vividly remembers the fear he felt every time his father was arrested while preaching at a Sunday service or teaching believers in their home in Communist Vietnam. Emmanuel would sometimes cling to his father's leg, trying to stop the police from taking him away.

And Emmanuel also remembers the loneliness and abandonment he felt while his father was imprisoned. Emmanuel resented his father's work, and that simmering anger didn't end when the government released his father from prison.

"I got angry with my father," Emmanuel says. "Sometimes I didn't even want to visit my father in prison."

Despite his father's boldness as a pastor, Emmanuel lacked confidence in his own faith. He often hid during church gatherings and youth events. "I was afraid somebody would ask me to pray or do something," he said. His face showed traces of his youthful shyness.

As a teenager, Emmanuel spent much of his free time lifting weights. It increased his confidence and helped him be less aggressive. But after years of traveling from province to province to compete in bodybuilding events, he realized the source of true strength wasn't his physique—it was his faith.

After attending a year-long Bible school in a major city, Emmanuel returned home and was appointed youth leader for more than four hundred children and teenagers at his church. Initially anxious about the work, he found peace through prayer as he accepted the new role. "I felt joy when I was with the youth, so sometimes I didn't want to go home," he said. "I wanted to be with the young people in the church."

Two years later, Emmanuel took advantage of his body-building background to serve as his father's bodyguard while he ministered in dangerous parts of Vietnam.

Emmanuel recalls an incident in the mountainous Central Highlands when he and his father narrowly escaped a trap set by robbers. The robbers had strung ropes to snare travelers' motor-bikes, but the ropes snapped and Emmanuel and his father escaped unharmed.

> "I DID NOT REALIZE THE IMPORTANCE OF MINISTRY."

During the six years he spent along-side his father, Emmanuel saw God work through his dad. "I did not realize the importance of ministry," he said. "I intended to go with my father to protect him and just do ordinary work, but later God showed me what I had been through was the way he was training me for my future in ministry."

Emmanuel's ministry mirrors his father's. He regularly visits villages to share the gospel. He's gone for days at a time, far from his wife and their young daughter.

Government authorities oppose Christians in Vietnam when they evangelize outside the church or conduct community events. Emmanuel has been confronted repeatedly by authorities about his ministry work.

Several years ago, police attempted to intimidate him by demanding that he report to the police station every day for two weeks. Today they still occasionally "investigate" his outreach efforts, especially when he and others minister to children.

The people he shares the gospel with and the persecution he's faced have helped Emmanuel better understand his childhood and view it in a new light. He has forgiven his father for those missed events and missing years.

"NOW I UNDERSTAND WHY MY FATHER SACRIFICED."

"Now I understand why my father sacrificed," he said. "I feel and understand the calling of God; that is why I am willing to do it. My ministry is the same as my father's before. I live more for him now."

When Emmanuel considers his father's legacy, he admires, more than ever, his father's faithfulness and devotion to the gospel. Many people from different tribes trusted in Christ because Emmanuel's father sacrificed time at home with his family to share the gospel with them. Emmanuel now understands that his temporal loss was their eternal gain.

Viewing his father's ministry through the lens of his own work, Emmanuel said he realizes the good his father did for the kingdom and his family.

"He left for us a good name," Emmanuel said, smiling. "He did not give us a lot of money or property, but he gave us a good name and good reputation. Whenever we go from place to place, people know him, appreciate him, respect him, and love him very much. He has been a good example to follow."

DAY 216

Luke 6:22–23

"Blessed are you when people hate you and when they exclude you and revile you and spurn your name as evil, on account of the Son of Man! Rejoice in that day, and leap for joy, for behold, your reward is great in heaven; for so their fathers did to the prophets."

Be "blessed" when others hate and exclude you? Yes—and Jesus even tells you to rejoice and leap for joy when that happens. He knew that if you're living kingdom values in a fallen world—if you're following him—you're headed into conflict. So be aware—but also go.

DAY 217

John 17:18

*"As you sent me into the world, so I
have sent them into the world."*

Lord, you've launched me into a life of purpose—to tell the world your good news. As I follow you, I know I'll encounter joy, be stretched beyond my limits, face fear, and meet you in both joy and pain. Lord, I know you are with me on this journey, but I pray that I will sense your presence. Guide me as I seek you in obedience. Amen.

DAY 218

Acts 19:8

And he entered the synagogue and for three months spoke boldly, reasoning and persuading them about the kingdom of God.

Pharisees at the synagogue considered Paul a traitor. But despite the danger, Paul went there daily for months. The synagogue was a vital place for Christ's message to be heard. What hard place is God calling you to share the Good News? It could be a relationship that seems difficult to cultivate with a neighbor, a coworker, or a family member. Ask God for guidance and courage to speak boldly and graciously for him.

DAY 219

Deuteronomy 1:29–30

Then I said to you, "Do not be in dread or afraid of them. The LORD your God who goes before you will himself fight for you, just as he did for you in Egypt before your eyes."

Santiago and his wife, Mariana, are accustomed to fear. They plant churches in Colombia's "red zones," areas controlled by guerrilla and paramilitary groups. These groups target Christians because they view Christians as a threat to their movements. Followers of Christ refuse to join the groups' violent cause. When one of their members becomes a Christian, they leave the group. Despite the danger and their own fear, Christians continue to share God's Word and shepherd churches. "What helps me continue is the desire in my heart," said Mariana, whose relatives have been killed by paramilitaries. "I don't care about threats; I don't care about violence. What fills me [with] the most joy is when I take people who are intimidated a Bible."

Be inspired by Santiago and Mariana to move forward in obedience to Christ today.

DAY 220

Ephesians 5:1–2

Therefore be imitators of God, as beloved children.
And walk in love, as Christ loved us and gave himself
up for us, a fragrant offering and sacrifice to God.

At seventeen years old, Soni was sold into slavery by her aunt. She spent three decades as a prostitute in India before a Nepali Christian helped her escape. The woman shared the gospel with Soni, and Soni joyfully accepted Christ's invitation of salvation. But once Soni returned home, her family did not accept her because she had been a prostitute. Even worse, she had become an "untouchable" as a Christian. "Everybody rejected me; Jesus was the only one who loved me," Soni said. "Please pray…that all my family will come to know Jesus," Soni said. "Because Jesus died not only for me, but also for them."

Whatever else God calls you to do, walk in love and embrace forgiveness.

DAY 221

Philippians 1:21–23, 27–29

*For to me to live is Christ, and to die is gain. If I am to live
in the flesh, that means fruitful labor for me....My desire is
to depart and be with Christ, for that is far better....Only
let your manner of life be worthy of the gospel of Christ,
so that whether I come and see you or am absent, I may
hear of you that you are standing firm in one spirit, with
one mind striving side by side for the faith of the gospel,
and not frightened in anything by your opponents....For
it has been granted to you that for the sake of Christ you
should not only believe in him but also suffer for his sake.*

Paul strove for fruitful labor, and he knew he would suffer. Paul did
not encourage believers to avoid either labor or suffering, but instead to be worthy of the gospel as they shared the Good News of Jesus
Christ. He encourages you to do the same.

DAY 222

Colossians 3:23–24

Whatever you do, work heartily, as for the Lord and not for men, knowing that from the Lord you will receive the inheritance as your reward. You are serving the Lord Christ.

L ord, the work you've called me to do is sometimes hard. At times I'm tempted to cut corners or ignore your calling. I repent of that disobedience. Solidify my commitment to you, and help me feel your encouragement as I work with you to bring your heavenly kingdom to earth. Lift my eyes from the tasks at hand to savor the inheritance you've promised. I want to serve you well with all I am, today and always. Amen.

DAY 223

Jeremiah 1:4–9

Now the word of the LORD came to me, saying, "Before I formed you in the womb I knew you, and before you were born I consecrated you; I appointed you a prophet to the nations." Then I said, "Ah, Lord GOD! Behold, I do not know how to speak, for I am only a youth." But the LORD said to me, "Do not say, 'I am only a youth'; for to all to whom I send you, you shall go, and whatever I command you, you shall speak. Do not be afraid of them, for I am with you to deliver you, declares the LORD." Then the LORD put out his hand and touched my mouth. And the LORD said to me, "Behold, I have put my words in your mouth."

Jeremiah was prepared to speak fearlessly because God literally put words in his mouth. The Holy Spirit gives you words as well. So be his bold witness—he is with you!

DAY 224

Matthew 25:21

His master said to him, "Well done, good and faithful
servant. You have been faithful over a little; I will set
you over much. Enter into the joy of your master."

One of Jatya's most prized possessions, a manila packet, is stuffed with photos and newspaper articles. The articles recount the eight times Jatya was beaten for sharing the gospel in his village in India. After each brutal beating, however, Jatya returned home from the hospital, grabbed his Bible, and headed back to his village. "Until my last breath," Jatya said, "I want to serve and live my life for Jesus."

How does Jatya's commitment to God's assignment inspire you to pursue faithfulness to God's assignment for you today?

DAY 225

Isaiah 61:1–4

*The Spirit of the Lord G*OD *is upon me, because the L*ORD
*has anointed me to bring good news to the poor; he has
sent me to bind up the brokenhearted, to proclaim liberty
to the captives, and the opening of the prison to those
who are bound; to proclaim the year of the L*ORD's *favor,
and the day of vengeance of our God; to comfort all who
mourn; to grant to those who mourn in Zion—to give them
a beautiful headdress instead of ashes, the oil of gladness
instead of mourning, the garment of praise instead of a
faint spirit; that they may be called oaks of righteousness,
the planting of the L*ORD, *that he may be glorified.*

The word "anointed" is used to describe the process of setting apart kings, priests, prophets, and…you. As a follower of Jesus, you're set apart to do the work he's calling you to do. And you can do it fearlessly, for he who has anointed you will sustain you in the face of any insecurity.

DAY 226

2 Timothy 1:8–9, 11–12

*Therefore do not be ashamed of the testimony about our
Lord, nor of me his prisoner, but share in suffering for the
gospel by the power of God, who saved us and called us to a
holy calling, not because of our works but because of his own
purpose and grace, which he gave us in Christ Jesus before
the ages began, . . . for which I was appointed a preacher
and apostle and teacher, which is why I suffer as I do.*

When Andres pursued God's calling on his life—to take the gospel to people living in some of the most dangerous areas of Colombia—his father tried to dissuade him. He placed money on the table and told Andres: "Here's half the money you'll need to buy a coffin . . . because we know that you are not coming back." Andres confidently replied, "If it pleases him that I die there, then I will die there. Christ gave his life for me, and I have to give my life for him."

Ministering among Your Enemies

Every morning at 4:45 a.m., Daniel Zagi and his wife, Victoria, awakened and prepared for another day of training new disciples. They began their morning in chapel, praising God alongside the men and women in their care. They dedicated the rest of the day to teaching the former Muslims how to live as new creations in Christ in Nigeria.

Daniel was uniquely qualified to mentor young Christians from Muslim backgrounds. While growing up in Nigeria's Bauchi state, Daniel wasn't treated well by his father's four Muslim wives. His biological mother was a Christian, however, and at the age of nineteen, Daniel came to faith in Jesus Christ. When he met Victoria through his church fellowship, the two married and began a life together; he knew she was a prayerful woman who was fully committed to the Lord.

In the late 1990s, Daniel felt the Lord calling him in a direction he didn't want to go. "I realized that the Lord was calling me to the Muslims," Daniel said. He would have preferred serving any other group of people. "Lord, if it is these people, forget about it," he prayed. "I would love to work with other people, not them." Then, while reading about Jesus' encounter with the Samaritan woman in John 4, Daniel saw how the relationship between Jews and Samaritans in Jesus' day resembled the relationship between Christians and Muslims in Nigeria.

So Daniel finally yielded to the idea of reaching out to Nigerian Muslims.

Deciding he'd work as an evangelist and church planter, Daniel began to share the gospel in small villages throughout Bauchi state. In one village, five people came to faith in Christ and asked Daniel to build them a church. He hired a recent Bible school graduate to pastor the church and paid the pastor out of his own pocket.

"I was so excited," Daniel said. But three weeks later, Daniel discovered the converts had reverted to Islam.

The new believers had no foundation to help them understand the pastor's teaching and no way of dealing with the persecution they experienced from their families and community. Daniel realized God was pointing him toward a new kind of ministry. "If you can't maintain, don't obtain," he sensed the Lord saying.

"I WOULD LOVE TO WORK WITH OTHER PEOPLE, NOT THEM."

Daniel understood that instead of taking the gospel to Muslims, he should focus on deep, personal care for new converts— even bringing them into his own home. With Victoria's consent, he brought seven new converts home with him.

Although three of the seven eventually gave up and left, the couple decided against adding to the number of new believers in their home until those still with them were well established in their faith. "By the grace of God, we sustained the four," Daniel said.

Their ministry became more effective once those first converts became well-grounded believers. "The work was easier for us because they were also helping us reach out," Daniel explained.

Within a few years, it became clear Daniel, Victoria, and the Christian converts needed to leave Bauchi state, which was quickly becoming an Islamist stronghold. Although they were unsure where to go, they trusted that God would direct them through prayer. And soon, Daniel had a vision of a gated facility with bunk beds and a classroom.

At the Holy Spirit's leading, the couple moved to Jos, a city on the dividing line between Nigeria's Muslim-majority north and Christian-majority south. Daniel and Victoria found a property matching Daniel's vision—a property with a gate, bunk beds, and a classroom.

God had provided. And for more than twenty years, their ministry work continued.

Throughout the years, Daniel received some surprising comments when he described his ministry. Once, a concerned Christian offered to help Daniel's family get asylum after he heard that Daniel and Victoria witnessed to Muslims in northern Nigeria. Daniel didn't hesitate to correct the well-intentioned believer.

"You think God made a mistake keeping me there in Nigeria?" Daniel asked. "If you want to pray for me, pray that the Lord will give us safety so that I can preach the gospel of Christ, . . . that we can stand this persecution . . . [and] work here for the Lord."

DAY 227

Acts 6:2–4, 7

And the twelve summoned the full number of the disciples and said, "It is not right that we should give up preaching the word of God to serve tables. Therefore, brothers, pick out from among you seven men of good repute, full of the Spirit and of wisdom, whom we will appoint to this duty. But we will devote ourselves to prayer and to the ministry of the word." And the word of God continued to increase, and the number of the disciples multiplied greatly in Jerusalem, and a great many of the priests became obedient to the faith.

Lord, please strengthen my persecuted brothers and sisters around the world. Give them a boldness that can only come from you. Calm their fears. Solidify their courage. Feed their faith. May they reflect you so brightly that the whole world sees the light of your love in their lives. Please show me how I can encourage persecuted Christians and those who serve you on dangerous and difficult mission fields. Amen.

DAY 228

Ephesians 3:7–10

*Of this gospel I was made a minister according to the
gift of God's grace, which was given me by the working
of his power. To me, though I am the very least of all the
saints, this grace was given, to preach to the Gentiles the
unsearchable riches of Christ, and to bring to light for
everyone what is the plan of the mystery hidden for ages
in God, who created all things, so that through the church
the manifold wisdom of God might now be made known
to the rulers and authorities in the heavenly places.*

It's both an honor and a responsibility to share the gospel. Jesus commissioned you and empowers you. God's grace is stronger than any fear you might have. Remember: your perfection isn't the issue, for God is perfect. Shine his light far and wide!

> We have had great joys. We have also had our anxieties. But if
> it is dangerous to do God's work, how much more dangerous
> it is to leave it undone.
>
> Sabina Wurmbrand

Matthew 5:13–16

*"You are the salt of the earth, but if salt has lost its taste,
how shall its saltiness be restored? It is no longer good for
anything except to be thrown out and trampled under
people's feet. You are the light of the world. A city set
on a hill cannot be hidden. Nor do people light a lamp
and put it under a basket, but on a stand, and it gives
light to all in the house. In the same way, let your light
shine before others, so that they may see your good works
and give glory to your Father who is in heaven."*

Is it salty? One taste and you'll know. And in a dark room, one flickering lamp makes a difference. Jesus Christ's purpose changes you—a change that affects everyone around you. Where might you add flavor to the world around you? Where is a dark place God wants you to shine?

DAY 230

Psalm 57:2

I cry out to God Most High, to God
who fulfills his purpose for me.

Thank you, Lord, for working in me, through me, and around me to further your kingdom on earth. I acknowledge you are the Most High God, and I give myself to fulfill your purpose according to your good pleasure. I cling to you, Holy One. Only you can strengthen and guide me as I fulfill the assignment you've given me. Amen.

DAY 231

Luke 5:9–10

*For he and all who were with him were astonished at the
catch of fish that they had taken, and so also were James
and John, sons of Zebedee, who were partners with Simon.
And Jesus said to Simon, "Do not be afraid; from now on
you will be catching men." And when they had brought
their boats to land, they left everything and followed him.*

What is God's assignment for you today? What fear do you need
to abandon in order to pursue it?

DAY 232

2 Corinthians 5:18–20

All this is from God, who through Christ reconciled us to himself and gave us the ministry of reconciliation; that is, in Christ God was reconciling the world to himself, not counting their trespasses against them, and entrusting to us the message of reconciliation. Therefore, we are ambassadors for Christ, God making his appeal through us.

Andrew, one of Jesus' twelve disciples, carried the message of reconciliation to the boundaries of the known world. One convert was a woman named Maximilla, the wife of a Roman high official who was so angry at his wife's conversion he threatened Andrew with death by crucifixion. To this, Andrew replied, "Had I feared the death of the cross, I should not have preached the majesty and gloriousness of Christ." Unwilling to recant his faith in Christ, Andrew was tied to an X-shaped cross to die a slow and painful death.

How does this story inspire you to press through fear to faithfully pursue the ministry of reconciliation with your family and community?

DAY 233

Ephesians 4:1–3

*I therefore, a prisoner for the Lord, urge you to walk
in a manner worthy of the calling to which you have
been called, with all humility and gentleness, with
patience, bearing with one another in love, eager to
maintain the unity of the Spirit in the bond of peace.*

Lord, I am eternally grateful you've adopted me into your family. As
a part of your family, I pray I take on your traits of humility, gentleness, patience, love, and peace. I fail often, and I'm sometimes afraid
even if I don't know why. When I fail, let me allow your strength to
shine. Where I am fearful, let your purpose give me boldness. May the
people who see me working see less of me—and more of you. Amen.

DAY 234

Exodus 3:11-12

But Moses said to God, "Who am I that I should go to
Pharaoh and bring the children of Israel out of Egypt?" He
said, "But I will be with you, and this shall be the sign
for you, that I have sent you: when you have brought the
people out of Egypt, you shall serve God on this mountain."

When Moses questioned God's assignment for him, the Lord responded with a promise: he would be with Moses. What assignments do you face today that necessitate the assurance of God's presence? List them below, beginning each task with this phrase: "God is with me today as I…"

_____

_____

_____

_____

WHOM SHALL I FEAR?

Our Obedience:
A Daily Choice

You have a choice to make today. It's the same choice that waits for you every day. Will you obey or not?

That's a crossroad disciples come to often because God doesn't hide what he expects from us. Jesus isn't shy about showing us, in Scripture, what it means to live in a way that pleases the Lord.

But it's up to you to decide if you'll choose to obey him.

Richard and Sabina daily faced the choice to obey as the Communists began to occupy their homeland of Romania. Richard knew that his life as a pastor, until that time, had been full of satisfaction. He had all he needed for his family. He had the trust and love of his parishioners. But he was not at peace. "Why was I allowed to live as usual, while a cruel dictatorship was destroying everything dear to me, and while others were suffering for their faith?" he asked. On many nights,

Sabina and Richard prayed together, asking God to let them bear the cross of Christ.

Richard's arrest, in the widespread roundups that were going on at that time, could be considered an answer to his prayer, Richard later said. However, he never would have guessed that the first man to join him in his cell would be Comrade Patrascanu, the man who brought Communism to power in Romania.

When the door of Richard's room in Calea Rahova prison opened to admit Patrascanu, Richard initially assumed that the official had come in person to question him. Why was I so honored? Richard wondered. Then the guards locked the door behind Patrascanu. Stranger still, Richard saw that his shirt was opened at the neck and he was without a tie. Richard looked down at his highly polished shoes—the laces were missing! Still, Richard obediently talked to him about Christ as he bore his cross in prison.

Biblical faith is costly and active—even to the point of sharing Christ with the very person who was responsible for ushering in an atheistic tyranny. Biblical faith requires Christians to choose to walk a narrow path, one that's often uphill. It not only leads to a beautiful place but also yields joy on the journey.

Advancing God's kingdom requires us to set aside our own agendas. It demands paying attention to what God calls us to do and then doing it. It means to accept God's assignments and fulfilling them, even if he doesn't explain what he's up to.

It's choosing.

It's choosing obedience every day.

DAY 235

Isaiah 52:7

How beautiful upon the mountains are the feet of
him who brings good news, who publishes peace,
who brings good news of happiness, who publishes
salvation, who says to Zion, "Your God reigns."

As a biblical disciple, yours are the beautiful feet that bring good news! Wherever you go—work, home, community gatherings, the store—you carry that good news with you. And you can carry it fearlessly, boldly, obediently. Your God reigns.

DAY 236

Acts 8:4–6

Now those who were scattered went about preaching the word. Philip went down to the city of Samaria and proclaimed to them the Christ. And the crowds with one accord paid attention to what was being said by Philip, when they heard him and saw the signs that he did.

After the Islamic Revolution, Soro and Ali fled Iran. But God never allowed them to lose their love for their countrymen. They responded to God's call to return and disciple the growing number of Iranian Christians. Despite harassment, arrest, and constant surveillance, this bold couple knew their obedience was a sacrifice worthy of Christ. "For us, it was so clear," Soro said. "The joy and privilege of being able to go overshadowed the fact that something could happen."

How does Soro and Ali's obedience inspire you to walk obediently with Christ today?

DAY 237

Romans 12:1–2

*I appeal to you therefore, brothers, by the mercies of God,
to present your bodies as a living sacrifice, holy and acceptable to God, which is your spiritual worship. Do not be
conformed to this world, but be transformed by the renewal
of your mind, that by testing you may discern what is the
will of God, what is good and acceptable and perfect.*

Biblical disciples place themselves on the altar of sacrifice each day
understanding there will be a price to pay for obedience. Bindi
and her husband followed Jesus and turned away from animistic and
Hindu beliefs in India. After her husband was killed because of his
bold witness, Bindi proclaimed, "I will live for Jesus or die for Jesus."

Will you make living for Jesus your own proclamation today?

DAY 238

Acts 9:10–17

*Now there was a disciple at Damascus named Ananias.
…And the Lord said to him, "Rise and go to the street
called Straight, and at the house of Judas look for a man of
Tarsus named Saul, for behold, he is praying, and he has
seen in a vision a man named Ananias come in and lay
his hands on him so that he might regain his sight." But
Ananias answered, "Lord, I have heard from many about
this man, how much evil he has done to your saints at
Jerusalem. And here he has authority from the chief priests
to bind all who call on your name." But the Lord said to
him, "Go, for he is a chosen instrument of mine to carry
my name before the Gentiles and kings and the children
of Israel.…" So Ananias departed and entered the house.*

Ananias chose to trust God's words rather than surrender to his fear. What words of God in Scripture do you find difficult to obey? How do you push through fear to obey Jesus Christ?

DAY 239

Hebrews 6:11-12

And we desire each one of you to show the same earnestness
to have the full assurance of hope until the end, so that
you may not be sluggish, but imitators of those who
through faith and patience inherit the promises.

S luggish" isn't a word you would like to describe your obedience to
God, but does the description fit? Or do you—eagerly and wholeheartedly—give yourself to serve God? How would someone who
watches you describe your willingness to walk faithfully in obedience?

DAY 240

1 Peter 1:13–16

Therefore, preparing your minds for action, and being sober-minded, set your hope fully on the grace that will be brought to you at the revelation of Jesus Christ. As obedient children, do not be conformed to the passions of your former ignorance, but as he who called you is holy, you also be holy in all your conduct, since it is written, "You shall be holy, for I am holy."

How freeing it is to know that through Christ, we can be holy! As Peter wrote, we no longer have to be conformed to the passions of our former ignorance. Obedience is a daily choice to turn our eyes to Christ. How will you submit your thoughts to his Lordship and find the freedom that comes from living as his obedient children?

It is written, "You shall be holy, for I am holy" (1 Peter 1:16). There exists in us the potential to be holy like God.

Richard Wurmbrand

DAY 241

Acts 4:31

And when they had prayed, the place in which
they were gathered together was shaken, and they
were all filled with the Holy Spirit and continued
to speak the word of God with boldness.

Mina, a Christian living and serving among her neighbors in Indonesia, is prompted to boldly share Christ when she hears the Muslim call to prayer played over a mosque's loudspeakers. Despite the opposition she faces, Mina trusts the Holy Spirit to ease the anger of those with whom she shares Christ.

Holy Spirit, fill me with boldness when I pray and obey. Amen.

DAY 242

Hebrews 11:23–28

By faith Moses, when he was born, was hidden for three months by his parents, because they saw that the child was beautiful, and they were not afraid of the king's edict. By faith Moses, when he was grown up, refused to be called the son of Pharaoh's daughter, choosing rather to be mistreated with the people of God than to enjoy the fleeting pleasures of sin. He considered the reproach of Christ greater wealth than the treasures of Egypt, for he was looking to the reward. By faith he left Egypt, not being afraid of the anger of the king, for he endured as seeing him who is invisible. By faith he kept the Passover and sprinkled the blood, so that the Destroyer of the firstborn might not touch them.

Every act of your obedience is rooted in faith. Like Moses, find confidence in God's ability to provide, sustain, and guide you. Because of your faith in God alone, you can walk through the veil of fear and pursue obedience to him. What step can you take today to demonstrate your faith in Jesus Christ?

DAY 243

Acts 20:17–19, 22–24

Now from Miletus he sent to Ephesus and called the elders of the church to come to him. And when they came to him, he said to them: "You yourselves know how I lived among you the whole time…serving the Lord with all humility and with tears and with trials that happened to me through the plots of the Jews; And now, behold, I am going to Jerusalem, constrained by the Spirit, not knowing what will happen to me there, except that the Holy Spirit testifies to me in every city that imprisonment and afflictions await me. But I do not account my life of any value nor as precious to myself, if only I may finish my course and the ministry that I received from the Lord Jesus, to testify to the gospel of the grace of God."

Paul knew the cost of a bold, obedient witness—and he paid it joyfully. What cost are you willing to pay to walk in obedience to God?

A Faithful Disobedience

Despite intense pressure from China's Communist government, Early Rain Covenant Church of Chengdu refused to give up practicing the Christian faith.

Early Rain started as a home Bible study and later became an independent church. The church refused to join the government-approved Three-Self Patriotic Movement (TSPM), a church movement established to ensure allegiance to the Communist government. And the church's refusal to join TSPM made Early Rain illegal and considered dangerous by the Chinese government.

From the outset, Early Rain was intentionally open about its worship and missional positions. The church published its sermons on the internet, printed weekly bulletins, and even posted its name on elevator buttons in the building where it met. The church's strategy was to hide nothing from the government and to hold fast to its convictions.

"The Bible teaches us that in all matters relating to the gospel and human conscience, we must obey God and not men," wrote Wang Yi, Early Rain's head pastor. "For this reason, spiritual disobedience and bodily suffering are both ways we testify to another, eternal world and to another, glorious King."

Early Rain was known among Chinese house churches for its emphasis on evangelism and mercy missions, both generally avoided by churches wanting to escape government notice. Church leaders also spoke out against abortion and denounced the TSPM for cooperating with the atheistic Chinese government.

In September of 2017, the Chinese State Council issued new regulations on the "Administration of Religious Affairs." In March of 2018, the TSPM and government-sanctioned China Christian Council launched a multi-year plan promoting the "Sinicization of Christianity."

Sinicization is the process of bringing everything under the influence of Chinese culture, which, in reality, means under the influence of Chinese communism. The plan proposed to rewrite biblical commentaries to introduce Buddhist and Confucian teachings into the Old Testament and provide commentary on the New Testament that drew parallels to socialism. It also advocated "incorporating Chinese features into church worship services, hymns and songs, clergy's attire, and the architectural style of church buildings."

> "THE BIBLE TEACHES US THAT ...WE MUST OBEY GOD AND NOT MEN."

With the enactment of these religious "reforms," churches that previously met openly in large groups were banned. Authorities closed one church after another and detained pastors, lawyers, and lay leaders—some of whom received fines and lengthy prison sentences.

Pastor Wang Yi was arrested. The government raided Early Rain offices and confiscated more than 10,000 Bibles, books, and CDs from the church's offices. Then church leaders prayerfully published "A Declaration for the Sake of the Christian Faith," which emphasized the supremacy of God, the authority and inerrancy of the Bible, and the role of the church. The document concluded with this bold statement: "For the sake of the gospel, we are prepared to bear all losses, even the loss of our freedom and our lives."

"FOR THE SAKE OF THE GOSPEL, WE ARE PREPARED TO BEAR ALL LOSSES..."

Pastor Wang Yi previously prepared the document with the understanding it would be published if he was detained for more than 48 hours. His name was first on the list of signatories. More than four hundred Chinese pastors signed the declaration, which publicly opposed the government's campaign against religious freedom.

"I firmly believe that Christ has called me to carry out this faithful disobedience through a life of service, under this regime that opposes the gospel and persecutes the church," Pastor Wang Yi wrote. "The goal of disobedience is not to change the world but to testify about another world."

He was sentenced to nine years in prison.

Despite ongoing, intense government attempts to force Early Rain's members to stop practicing their faith, the members continued to worship God. Worship services moved online. Small groups continued to meet. Evangelism continued. A faithful witness still shined brightly.

WHOM SHALL I FEAR?

The government shows no sign of backing away from its plan to Sinicize Christianity. More arrests, raids, church closings, and even demolitions of church buildings occur each month.

Yet many Chinese believers, like those at Early Rain Covenant Church of Chengdu, are prepared to confront persecution through sound teaching and the work of the Holy Spirit.

In the words of an Early Rain church elder, "May the whole world know that we are joyfully willing to receive this persecution for the sake of our faith."

DAY 244

Ezekiel 2:5–6

*"And whether they hear or refuse to hear (for they
are a rebellious house) they will know that a prophet
has been among them. And you, son of man, be not
afraid of them, nor be afraid of their words, though
briers and thorns are with you and you sit on scor-
pions. Be not afraid of their words, nor be dismayed
at their looks, for they are a rebellious house."*

Are you afraid of other people's words? Of what they'll say to you or about you? Fear not—you're not called to win arguments or impress others with elegant language. Instead, you're called to share the good news with those who are willing to hear it. The Lord commanded Ezekiel to be unafraid of other people in this passage, and he asks the same of you.

DAY 245

Acts 5:27–29

And when they had brought them, they set them before the council. And the high priest questioned them, saying, "We strictly charged you not to teach in this name, yet here you have filled Jerusalem with your teaching, and you intend to bring this man's blood upon us." But Peter and the apostles answered, "We must obey God rather than men."

What a moment! Peter and the apostles must have been afraid as they faced the council, but they chose to obey God first and man second. What does obeying God, rather than others, look like in your life today?

DAY 246

Mark 5:35–36

While he was still speaking, there came from the ruler's house some who said, "Your daughter is dead. Why trouble the Teacher any further?" But overhearing what they said, Jesus said to the ruler of the synagogue, "Do not fear, only believe."

Obedience begins with a belief in God and his mighty power. Acknowledge your belief in him by praising him today. Write your words of praise to him below.

_____

_____

_____

_____

_____

DAY 247

1 Peter 4:12, 16

Beloved, do not be surprised at the fiery trial when it comes upon you to test you, as though something strange were happening to you. Yet if anyone suffers as a Christian, let him not be ashamed, but let him glorify God in that name.

Why do we care so much about what others think of us? Only one opinion ultimately matters—that of the Lord. So don't be afraid or ashamed to boldly obey God. Any scorn or scars that come to you are marks of faithfulness and a testimony of God's glory.

DAY 248

John 15:18–20

"If the world hates you, know that it has hated me before it hated you. If you were of the world, the world would love you as its own; but because you are not of the world, but I chose you out of the world, therefore the world hates you. Remember the word that I said to you: 'A servant is not greater than his master.' If they persecuted me, they will also persecute you. If they kept my word, they will also keep yours."

Expect persecution. That's the message Jesus gave to his first disciples, and it's still true today. As you live an obedient life, you can expect pushback from friends, colleagues, and the culture. If you expect persecution, you'll be prepared when persecution occurs. Are you being a witness today? Be obedient to God and prepare for opposition.

DAY 249

Acts 5:35, 38–42

And he said to them, "Men of Israel, take care what you
are about to do with these men....Keep away from these
men and let them alone, for if this plan or this undertaking
is of man, it will fail; but if it is of God, you will not be
able to overthrow them. You might even be found opposing
God!" So they took his advice, and when they had called
in the apostles, they beat them and charged them not to
speak in the name of Jesus, and let them go. Then they
left the presence of the council, rejoicing that they were
counted worthy to suffer dishonor for the name. And every
day, in the temple and from house to house, they did not
cease teaching and preaching that the Christ is Jesus.

How does the response of the apostles—who rejoiced when they
were counted worthy to suffer dishonor for the name of Jesus—
inspire you to be bold in the face of opposition?

DAY 250

Romans 12:19–21

"Beloved, never avenge yourselves, but leave it to the wrath of God, for it is written, 'Vengeance is mine, I will repay, says the Lord.' To the contrary, 'if your enemy is hungry, feed him; if he is thirsty, give him something to drink; for by so doing you will heap burning coals on his head.' Do not be overcome by evil, but overcome evil with good."

It's natural to fear others who intend to harm or harass us. Despite our fear of them, God calls us, through his power, to willingly show his love to our enemies. Who do you fear? How can you serve them as you share the love of your Father?

DAY 251

Philippians 4:9

What you have learned and received and
heard and seen in me—practice these things,
and the God of peace will be with you.

Our persecuted Christian family members are tremendous examples of taking one step of obedience, often at the risk of greater
peril. What they learn and receive from God's Word and from their
church leaders, they put into practice. God promises his peace as we
live in obedience.

Heavenly Father, I commit today to live out what I already know to
do. Thank you for the provision of your peace. Amen.

> Our mission gives to the Christians of the free world the
> example of Christian lives unbroken by sufferings. In suffer-
> ing, they love their torturers and are concerned about their
> souls.
>
> Richard Wurmbrand

DAY 252

Colossians 2:6–7

Therefore, as you received Christ Jesus the Lord, so walk in him, rooted and built up in him and established in the faith, just as you were taught, abounding in thanksgiving.

How did you receive salvation in Christ? Who first shared the gospel with you? Pause and thank God for the willing witness who led you to life in Christ. Then consider who you can share the good news with today.

DAY 253

1 Peter 2:15–17, 21

For this is the will of God, that by doing good you should put to silence the ignorance of foolish people. Live as people who are free, not using your freedom as a cover-up for evil, but living as servants of God. Honor everyone. Love the brotherhood. Fear God. Honor the emperor. For to this you have been called, because Christ also suffered for you, leaving you an example, so that you might follow in his steps.

F reedom in Christ results in living as a servant of God instead of demanding your own way. Who do you serve today? The truth is you're either serving God or someone else—and the way to life is found only in him. So live in freedom as a fearless, biblical, and fully devoted disciple.

DAY 254

2 Timothy 3:10–13

You, however, have followed my teaching, my conduct, my aim in life, my faith, my patience, my love, my steadfastness, my persecutions and sufferings that happened to me at Antioch, at Iconium, and at Lystra—which persecutions I endured; yet from them all the Lord rescued me. Indeed, all who desire to live a godly life in Christ Jesus will be persecuted, while evil people and impostors will go on from bad to worse, deceiving and being deceived.

After twelve years of hating Christians, Baluan reached a crossroads of belief. After his sister became a Christian, he saw her life transformed. He too sought truth and found it in Jesus Christ. Now Baluan boldly shares Christ and disciples those who respond to the gospel despite opposition from his family and community in Central Asia.

How can you follow God's instruction to proclaim the gospel today? As you walk in obedience to Jesus Christ, opposition may occur, but your joy will overcome all anxiety.

DAY 255

Hebrews 13:12–13

*So Jesus also suffered outside the gate in order to sanctify
the people through his own blood. Therefore let us go to
him outside the camp and bear the reproach he endured.*

Lord, you suffered abuse from the very people you came to save.
You felt their scorn, wiped their spit from your face, and endured
their fists and fury. I know I may one day be called to face what you
faced as I follow in your footsteps. Protect me from compromise, Lord.
Give me courage to press through fear to suffer for you. Amen.

A Costly Ministry

They come to him from all over Egypt, seeking baptism. Krystafer, an Orthodox Church leader, longed to reach Muslims for Christ even before he became a priest in 2006. He prayed that he'd be like Paul, reaching the nations.

"I was praying for Muslims in Egypt, Iran, Turkey, Saudi Arabia, [and] Syria," he said. "I didn't choose this ministry because I hate Islam. I love Muslims; I want them to know Jesus, especially those in Egypt."

Egyptian Orthodox (Coptic) Christians trace their lineage to the first-century ministry of Mark, which predates the founding of Islam. Composing roughly 10 percent of Egypt's population today, they face intense discrimination from majority Muslims. Coptic Christian girls are routinely kidnapped and forced to marry a Muslim man and then convert to Islam. Occasionally, Islamists attack churches or kill groups of Christians.

In this oppressive environment, most Copts keep to their own communities. Few share the gospel with Muslims. Fewer still are willing to baptize Muslims when they desire to be baptized in obedience to following Christ.

Yet such baptisms are taking place.

"What brings joy to my heart is when I baptize a former Muslim, and he is excited to be able to bring his family or friends to be baptized," Krystafer says. Baptizing former Muslims isn't something most Coptic priests do, but Krystafer sees his work as fulfilling Jesus' Great Commission. And this has resulted in pressure and threats from the national security police and Muslim extremists.

Yet Krystafer continues to baptize any new believer who asks him. And other Christian leaders across Egypt who lead Muslims to Christ but are afraid to baptize them know where to send the new believers.

Once when a fanatical Muslim came looking for Krystafer, church leaders protected him by directing the man elsewhere. "They are not able to do what I am doing," Krystafer explains, "but they are very happy to let me be full-time for this ministry because they believe in the ministry, though they are afraid to do it."

"JESUS HAS GIVEN ME THIS MINISTRY. HE GIVES ME THE COURAGE."

Frequently summoned to the national security police headquarters, a top official told him that he could not promise the priest that he would be protected from fanatics. "I don't listen," Krystafer said. "I don't get afraid."

Believers who come to Krystafer for baptism also face consequences. After Krystafer baptized a young mother and her two children, police spent five hours trying to persuade the woman to return to Islam. They also tried to get her to incriminate Krystafer.

To the authorities' surprise, she told them that she'd asked Krystafer to baptize her. The authorities then required her to attend five hours of Islamic instruction from an imam each week.

After that, a policeman warned her that if she didn't renounce her Christian faith, her children would be given to her ex-husband, and she'd never see them again.

Amid the risks, Krystafer approaches his ministry work with care, but not fear. "Jesus has given me this ministry," he said. "He gives me the courage. He gives me the peace to do it. He gives me the capability to do it. When he gives us a ministry in our life, we are responsible for what it costs us."

DAY 256

James 1:2–4

Count it all joy, my brothers, when you meet trials of various kinds, for you know that the testing of your faith produces steadfastness. And let steadfastness have its full effect, that you may be perfect and complete, lacking in nothing.

China has more than 200 million surveillance cameras throughout the country—enough for one camera per every seven citizens. The country also uses sophisticated facial recognition technology to track citizens. One church leader said, "Persecution itself is evil to the people of God, but we rejoice that the gospel can be spread." How is your faith being tested today? Flee fear and count that testing as joy, that you may be perfect and complete in Jesus Christ.

DAY 257

1 Peter 3:14–17

But even if you should suffer for righteousness' sake, you will be blessed. Have no fear of them, nor be troubled, but in your hearts honor Christ the Lord as holy, always being prepared to make a defense to anyone who asks you for a reason for the hope that is in you; yet do it with gentleness and respect, having a good conscience, so that, when you are slandered, those who revile your good behavior in Christ may be put to shame. For it is better to suffer for doing good, if that should be God's will, than for doing evil.

When you add heat, water will eventually reach a boiling point. When we face persecution, our faith passes through the fire. A lack of fear, a joyful heart, and an untroubled mind are some signs that you honor Christ despite your suffering. Take a moment and check these three attitudes, and commit to the Lord today that you will pursue them.

WHOM SHALL I FEAR?

DAY 258

1 John 2:2–3

*He is the propitiation for our sins, and not for
ours only but also for the sins of the whole world.
And by this we know that we have come to
know him, if we keep his commandments.*

Our persecuted Christian family chooses every day to obey God rather than men regardless of the price they will pay for that choice. Who are we obeying? The one who provided redemption through his one and only son, Jesus, the sacrifice for our sins. He is able!

DAY 259

Acts 4:12–13, 19–20

[Peter said,] "And there is salvation in no one else, for there is no other name under heaven given among men by which we must be saved." Now when they saw the boldness of Peter and John, and perceived that they were uneducated, common men, they were astonished. And they recognized that they had been with Jesus. But Peter and John answered them, "Whether it is right in the sight of God to listen to you rather than to God, you must judge, for we cannot but speak of what we have seen and heard."

Lord, it lifts my heart to know you use everyone who willingly obeys you. Formal theological training, status, or a heritage of faith aren't essential. Only intimacy with your Son is essential. I want to be known as one who's been with you. I want to give bold, fearless testimony of your faithfulness. Transform my heart so that it beats first and foremost for you. Transform my mind so I see the world as you see it. Prepare me to speak fearlessly for you. Amen.

WHOM SHALL I FEAR?

DAY 260

Revelation 2:9–10

"I know your tribulation and your poverty (but you are rich) and the slander of those who say that they are Jews and are not, but are a synagogue of Satan. Do not fear what you are about to suffer. Behold, the devil is about to throw some of you into prison, that you may be tested, and for ten days you will have tribulation. Be faithful unto death, and I will give you the crown of life."

Our persecuted Christian brothers and sisters who advance the gospel in hostile areas and restricted nations know this: Sometimes fear is a test. It can cause us to doubt God and turn from him. But a crown of life awaits those who remain faithful. Keep your eyes on your Father!

DAY 261

Revelation 12:10–11

And I heard a loud voice in heaven, saying, "Now the salvation and the power and the kingdom of our God and the authority of his Christ have come, for the accuser of our brothers has been thrown down, who accuses them day and night before our God. And they have conquered him by the blood of the Lamb and by the word of their testimony, for they loved not their lives even unto death."

Lord, I'm thankful for every gift my senses bring me and for every moment I'm alive. But I love you more than these gifts, Lord. You gave me this life, and I give it back to you to use however you wish. Please give me the courage to walk fearlessly in obedience to you all my days. Amen.

> I had learned in the Bible that Christians must suffer for the faith, so I thought, "Well, here it is," and I made my witness stronger. I shared Christ with them.
>
> Laila, a Christian in Central Asia who
> shared the gospel with her persecutors

WHOM SHALL I FEAR?

DAY 262

1 John 1:6–7

If we say we have fellowship with him while we walk in darkness, we lie and do not practice the truth. But if we walk in the light, as he is in the light, we have fellowship with one another, and the blood of Jesus his Son cleanses us from all sin.

Living a hidden life is living a lie. The light of Christ illuminates a path of obedience and purpose; the shadows hold only heartache. If you fear being fully known, accept that as a call to move into the light. The light will scorch your fear and blossom your joy.

DAY 263

Romans 6:16

*Do you not know that if you present yourselves to
anyone as obedient slaves, you are slaves of the one
whom you obey, either of sin, which leads to death,
or of obedience, which leads to righteousness?*

You're a slave of the one you obey and who has power in your life. Are you a slave to anxiety? To insecurity? To doubt? To fear? Ask the Lord to free you from any slavery that binds you so you can live in righteousness and obedience to him.

DAY 264

Hebrews 12:1–3

*Therefore, since we are surrounded by so great a cloud
of witnesses, let us also lay aside every weight, and sin
which clings so closely, and let us run with endurance
the race that is set before us, looking to Jesus, the founder
and perfecter of our faith, who for the joy that was set
before him endured the cross, despising the shame, and is
seated at the right hand of the throne of God. Consider
him who endured from sinners such hostility against
himself, so that you may not grow weary or fainthearted.*

Lord, thank you for Jesus and for what he accomplished on the
cross. Thank you for the victory that is found in Jesus Christ our
Lord. You alone are worthy of my loyalty and obedience. You alone can
guide and sustain me. May I never grow weary of serving you, Lord!
Amen.

God's Word:
Our Firm Foundation

People read the Bible for a variety of reasons. For some, it's a duty; for others, a habit. Some are just curious. The Bible overflows with amazing stories of God's revelation of himself to us.

But disciples read the Bible for another reason: To spend time with God. They find not just words but living words. Words that can—and do—transform their lives.

In the Bible, God shares what he most wants you to know about himself, about yourself, and about navigating the world. It's a place God reveals his nature and character, his values and priorities.

And the Bible is where you meet Jesus Christ our Lord, whose power and authority put a check on fear. You see that God's love never fails, and that his commitment to you never wavers. He is the rock on which you can build your life, and the shelter in which you can weather any storm.

For Sabina Wurmbrand, the Bible verses she memorized sustained her life during her sentence to hard labor in Communist Romania. Sabina told the story of women who, after their workday, would go to religious prisoners and ask, and even beg, to be told something of what they remembered from the Bible. The words from the Bible gave hope, comfort, and life.

Sabina had no Bible in the labor camp and wished she had learned more of it by heart as the Christians imprisoned with her hungered for it more than bread. The passages they did know by heart they repeated every day and every night when they held prayer vigils. Some Christians, like Sabina, had deliberately committed long passages of Scripture to memory, knowing that soon their turn would come to be arrested. These women brought riches with them to prison.

THE BETTER YOU KNOW GOD'S WORD, THE LESS ROOM FEAR HAS TO FIND ITS WAY INTO YOUR HEART.

While other prisoners quarreled and fought, they lay on their mattresses and prayed through the Bible. They meditated on the verses through the long nights. The Christians learned which parts of the Bible newcomers to the jail brought with them and would teach them the stories of the Bible they remembered. In this way, an unwritten Bible circulated through all of Romania's prisons.

Each of us needs the hope we can find only in God's Word. His Word sustains us because we all face dark days. The better you know God's Word, the less room fear has to find its way into your heart. The deeper his truths soak into you, the firmer your faith's foundation.

So come to God's Word expecting to encounter him there. Look for him to draw you near, hold you close, and then launch you into life, carrying his grace with you. If God's Word spoke to Sabina Wurmbrand in a cold, damp prison camp, his Word will most assuredly speak to you wherever you are.

When you open your Bible, you're not alone. God waits to meet you there.

DAY 265

1 Peter 1:22–25

*Having purified your souls by your obedience to the truth
for a sincere brotherly love, love one another earnestly
from a pure heart, since you have been born again, not
of perishable seed but of imperishable, through the living
and abiding word of God; for "All flesh is like grass and
all its glory like the flower of grass. The grass withers, and
the flower falls, but the word of the Lord remains forever."
And this word is the good news that was preached to you.*

Boun spent more than ten years in a Laotian prison for his bold and faithful witness. Enduring the first years was difficult because of the harsh conditions and because Boun desperately needed his Bible. Although his physical self wasted away behind bars, Boun's spiritual life flourished because he smuggled a Bible into his cell.

How is your spiritual life enriched by the Word of God today?

DAY 266

Psalm 119:105, 114

Your word is a lamp to my feet and a light to my path. You
are my hiding place and my shield; I hope in your word.

Are you walking through shadows today? Cling to the Word of
God as a light that will help you walk through fear, anxiety, or
insecurity. Write out a prayer to the Lord below, and ask him to lead
you. Then, follow him in bold obedience into a place of peace.

DAY 267

John 8:31–32

So Jesus said to the Jews who had believed him, "If you abide in my word, you are truly my disciples, and you will know the truth, and the truth will set you free."

Jesus shares a powerful formula for freedom: Abide in him as his faithful disciple, and you'll know the truth—and that truth will set you free. There are two actions that every biblical disciple can take responsibility for—abiding in God's Word and knowing the truth. The results of that effort will give Christians great freedom. And freedom replaces fear.

DAY 268

Proverbs 30:5

Every word of God proves true; he is a shield
to those who take refuge in him.

Every word, Lord—every word you speak is true! I trust and praise
you with my whole heart. Your ways are mighty, and your integrity is absolute. You never waver, your love for me doesn't fade, and you
don't forget your promises. You are Truth, Holy One! Amen.

> If you are not willing to die for what is in the Bible, you
> should not give money for Bibles. Because if you give, we will
> smuggle more Bibles. And if we smuggle more Bibles, there
> will be more martyrs.
>
> Richard Wurmbrand

DAY 269

Colossians 3:16

Let the word of Christ dwell in you richly, teach-
ing and admonishing one another in all wisdom,
singing psalms and hymns and spiritual songs,
with thankfulness in your hearts to God.

Notice the order in this passage: First, let the Word of Christ dwell richly in you and then—and only then—teach and admonish others. If you skip the first step, you will end up a Pharisee—concerned only with outward things and lacking love. Embrace God's Word, let it change you, and then teach and admonish one another with the Word.

DAY 270

Isaiah 40:8

The grass withers, the flower fades, but the word of our God will stand forever.

God's Word stands forever—and he has promised his presence. How does that help you face your fears today? Write down several promises from God's Word that the Lord brings to your mind. Think about each of them for a moment today. Allow his truth to replace all of your fears with his promises.

_____

_____

_____

_____

_____

_____

DAY 271

John 17:14, 17

"I have given them your word, and the world has hated them because they are not of the world, just as I am not of the world. Sanctify them in the truth; your word is truth."

Lord, your Word is true regardless of what the world says. Thank you for giving us your Word because in it, I meet you. I see your nature and experience your love. I praise you that your truth has changed me and continues to change me each day. Lord, thank you for this gift! Thank you for the power of your Word! Amen.

DAY 272

Psalm 1:1–4

*Blessed is the man who walks not in the counsel of the
wicked, nor stands in the way of sinners, nor sits in the seat
of scoffers; but his delight is in the law of the LORD, and on
his law he meditates day and night. He is like a tree planted
by streams of water that yields its fruit in its season, and
its leaf does not wither. In all that he does, he prospers.*

What does it mean to delight in the law of the Lord? As you think
on his Word, that daily discipline can turn your anxiety into
delight. May your new attitude of delight lead you toward keeping his
Word!

DAY 273

Luke 10:39–42

*And she had a sister called Mary, who sat at the Lord's feet
and listened to his teaching. But Martha was distracted
with much serving. And she went up to him and said,
"Lord, do you not care that my sister has left me to serve
alone? Tell her then to help me." But the Lord answered
her, "Martha, Martha, you are anxious and troubled about
many things, but one thing is necessary. Mary has chosen
the good portion, which will not be taken away from her."*

Our anxiety often drives us to frantically try to "fix" whatever
makes us uncomfortable. It's wisest to begin the day by simply
sitting at Jesus' feet and listening to his Word. Today, are you anxious,
or are you secure in his Word?

The Hand-Copied Bible

As a child, Gao Shao Xiu of China lived in constant pain. Doctors diagnosed her with inflammation of the brain. (She later learned it was liver damage.) The doctors told her parents not to invest much money or education in her because she wouldn't live that long.

But Gao's parents loved her deeply and sought help for her at one hospital after another for ten years.

When Gao was fifteen years old, a man persuaded her parents that he could heal her in three months, and he moved into the family home. But one night, he disappeared with all of the funds Gao's parents had given him.

Gao's hope of being free from pain faded again, and her parents began to plan her funeral. "I was patiently waiting to die," she said. Then two Christians who'd heard of Gao's situation traveled more than thirty miles to visit Gao and her family. They shared the gospel with the family and described a living God who could heal Gao.

"My father was skeptical after the quack doctor," Gao remembered, "but he allowed them to stay anyway." Instead of asking for money, the Christians prayed for three days. And for the first time in Gao's life, she was free of pain.

"It was then my father chose to believe in the Lord," she said, "and he publicly dedicated me to God." A short time later, Gao also placed her trust in Christ.

Gao and her family began to attend an illegal house church, but Bibles were scarce, and they'd never even seen an entire copy. The house church only had a few hand-copied chapters of the Bible that had been passed along. Since Gao had missed a lot of school as a child, she decided to advance her education by hand-copying the church's Bible chapters. She discovered that the more chapters of the Bible she copied, the healthier she grew.

Over time, her church acquired more Bible portions and eventually had a complete Bible. Gao continued to meticulously hand-copy the Bible, character by character.

When Communist Chairman Mao Zedong launched the Cultural Revolution in 1966, Gao was one of the many Chinese Christians persecuted for her faith. At one point, she was tied up and marched through the streets with a sign on her chest that said "anti-government."

"THANK YOU TO THOSE WHO PROVIDE THE WORDS OF LIFE TO CHRISTIANS HERE IN CHINA."

"I did not renounce my God," she said. "I knew he was real, he was powerful, and because of him, I was not dead."

Copying the Bible had firmly grounded Gao in the truths of Scripture. "In God's Word, I found truth, life itself, and clear guidance to the path I should be on," she said.

Now in her eighties, Gao continues to serve as a preacher and church leader. She also trains students throughout China.

"Our people meet in the church every day," she said. "I preach at least five times per week. Though I have committed many verses to memory, my favorite verse is still John 3:16. God's love is shown in that he chose me to be his spokesperson in China."

Gao continues the discipline of hand-copying passages of Scripture, as God's Word has been a constant anchor throughout her life. "Today, this same book is the most vital resource in my life," she said. "Thank you to those who provide the words of life to Christians here in China."

DAY 274

Isaiah 55:11

*"So shall my word be that goes out from my mouth; it shall
not return to me empty, but it shall accomplish that which I
purpose, and shall succeed in the thing for which I sent it."*

Shakeel and his family were Muslims who shared a home with a
Christian family in Pakistan. A Christian worker regularly visited the Christian family and was introduced to Shakeel's family. The
worker prayed for the Muslim family, and they felt moved and peaceful during his prayer. The Christian worker gave them an Urdu Bible,
and their teenage son read it to them. After some time, Shakeel told
the Christian worker that he wanted to place his trust in Jesus Christ
as Lord.

As bearers of the Word of God, when we faithfully speak its truth,
we spread Good News that transforms lives—like Shakeel's life was
changed. What a privilege to carry a message of hope to a hopeless
world and healing words to broken people! Thank God today for the
honor of speaking for him!

DAY 275

Matthew 4:3–4

And the tempter came and said to him, "If you are the Son of God, command these stones to become loaves of bread." But he answered, "It is written, "'Man shall not live by bread alone, but by every word that comes from the mouth of God.'"

The tempter, Satan, is a liar. He fights you with words. He needles you with doubt. Do as Jesus did when you encounter Satan's lies: Speak aloud the truth of God's Word. It's your shield and defense against the tempter's lies.

DAY 276

John 15:1, 4–6, 8–10

"I am the true vine, and my Father is the vinedresser. Abide in me, and I in you. As the branch cannot bear fruit by itself, unless it abides in the vine, neither can you, unless you abide in me. I am the vine; you are the branches. Whoever abides in me and I in him, he it is that bears much fruit, for apart from me you can do nothing. If anyone does not abide in me he is thrown away like a branch and withers; and the branches are gathered, thrown into the fire, and burned. By this my Father is glorified, that you bear much fruit and so prove to be my disciples. As the Father has loved me, so have I loved you. Abide in my love. If you keep my commandments, you will abide in my love, just as I have kept my Father's commandments and abide in his love."

Lord, show me what to glean from this passage today. Help me bear fruit through your vine.

DAY 277

Psalm 19:7–8

*The law of the LORD is perfect, reviving the soul; the
testimony of the LORD is sure, making wise the simple;
the precepts of the LORD are right, rejoicing the heart; the
commandment of the LORD is pure, enlightening the eyes.*

Quick: List every perfect thing in your life. Short list, isn't it? Here's
one: God's Word. Open your Bible today. The life-giving Word of
Truth can fill you with confidence as you face the uncertainty of today.

WHOM SHALL I FEAR?

DAY 278

2 Timothy 2:8–10

Remember Jesus Christ, risen from the dead, the offspring of David, as preached in my gospel, for which I am suffering, bound with chains as a criminal. But the word of God is not bound! Therefore I endure everything for the sake of the elect, that they also may obtain the salvation that is in Christ Jesus with eternal glory.

Paul's wrists were rubbed raw by chains. He was a prisoner. But what Paul carried with him—God's Word—wasn't bound. It set Paul free even though he was in captivity. Though you may feel shackled by shame and fear or bound by burdens, God's Word can also set you free. Ask him to show you freedom through his Word today.

DAY 279

Matthew 24:35

*"Heaven and earth will pass away, but
my words will not pass away."*

Lord, all that's around me in this life will fade except for you and your Word. Since I stand with you, I stand where I cannot be shaken and where your powerful arm will sustain me. I praise you, Lord. I give myself to you and cling to your promises. Amen.

DAY 280

Proverbs 2:1-5

My son, if you receive my words and treasure up my commandments with you, making your ear attentive to wisdom and inclining your heart to understanding; yes, if you call out for insight and raise your voice for understanding, if you seek it like silver and search for it as for hidden treasures, then you will understand the fear of the Lord and find the knowledge of God.

Lord, I open my heart to you. I listen for your wisdom, and I'm ready to hear and obey you. Guide me to the specific truth I need from your Word today, Lord. Protect me from anything that would distract me from you. Fear, insecurity, anxiety, doubt—I lay them aside so I can walk in obedience. May I cling as tightly to you as you cling to me. Amen.

DAY 281

Philippians 2:14–16

Do all things without grumbling or disputing, that you may be blameless and innocent, children of God without blemish in the midst of a crooked and twisted generation, among whom you shine as lights in the world, holding fast to the word of life, so that in the day of Christ I may be proud that I did not run in vain or labor in vain.

When Poonam quietly left Hinduism, the Bible she obtained became her most prized possession. The young Indian wife and mother of three secretly read God's Word every day and grew in her understanding of God's love for her. But she feared that her husband would find out about her new faith, and soon, he did. One day, he overheard her speaking a Christian prayer. Then he found her Bible and angrily tore it to pieces and kicked her out of the home. After local Christians replaced her Bible, Poonam said, "My Bible is everything to me; without it, I can't live."

How closely do you hold God's Word?

DAY 282

Psalm 130:5

I wait for the Lord, my soul waits, and in his word I hope.

Desperate and hopeless, Fariba decided to commit suicide because she felt worthless. After she bought the pills to end her life, she rode a bus when a woman sat next to her. The woman handed her a book. Fariba tried to refuse it, but the woman told her that it was a gift from God. She wanted Fariba to know that he loved her and cared about her. Moved by the stranger's kindness, Fariba decided to read the book. She found peace with God through it. "I was hopeless and disheartened, and I wanted to end my life by killing myself, but God had a plan for me," she said. "He found me; he saved my life. Please pray for me that I can share the gospel with other women who need to find their identity in Christ."

How does Fariba's story inspire you to walk fearlessly today?

Sharing God's Word in
the Depths of "Hell"

As Pastor Houmayoun led a prayer meeting at his home in Shiraz, Iran, secret police stormed in and arrested him, his wife, their seventeen-year-old son, and four other church leaders.

The seven Christians were blindfolded and taken to an intelligence prison for questioning. After days of interrogation, they were moved to a public prison and ordered to keep quiet about why they were arrested; the guards rightly feared the spread of Christianity among the prison's six thousand prisoners. But Houmayoun and the other believers felt compelled to obey a higher authority.

"It would have been comfortable just to be quiet and not talk about Jesus," Houmayoun says. "Things would have gone better for us in prison."

As they shared the gospel with their Muslim inmates, one thing became clear: They were going to need Bibles.

The Christians wrote memorized Bible verses on any paper they could find. "During the times when we were under pressure," Houmayoun said, "God was reminding us of these verses and strengthening us through the parts that we memorized."

After thirty-seven days, Houmayoun's son was released from prison. Seven months later, Houmayoun's wife was also released. When the five Christians remaining in prison were finally allowed to call family and friends, the prisoners asked those friends to write down chapters of Scripture in English and give them to an imam (an Islamic leader) who visited prisoners regularly. Neither the imam nor the guards could read English, so they couldn't read the "letters" from friends.

Christians who could read English then translated the Scripture into Farsi. Within months, the believers had complete, handwritten copies of some books of the Bible to read and share. And as they continued to receive new chapters, they made additional copies.

"GOD WAS REMINDING US OF THESE VERSES…"

While Bibles were highly restricted outside the prison, inside, they multiplied. The Bibles inspired more evangelism, which angered the guards even more. They separated the Christians with the hope of hindering their evangelistic work, but the plan backfired. Each believer had a handwritten Bible, disguised as a simple diary, to take with him.

"We didn't have access to all of [the prisoners] in the beginning, but because they kept punishing us, they were moving us from the better part of the jail to the worst part of the jail," Houmayoun said. "Because of this, we had access to most of the jail."

For several months, Houmayoun continued to share the love of Jesus and the truths of Scripture with Muslims in his new cell. But as guards saw prisoners responding to his evangelism, they grew increasingly frustrated and finally moved him to the harshest part of the prison known as Hell.

There, in the prison's basement, two hundred violent prisoners served life sentences or awaited hanging. Inmates made knives from cans to protect themselves. Murders occurred every week. Bloodstains on Houmayoun's sleeping mat and blanket were a graphic reminder of the constant violence.

Two years after their arrest, five months of which Houmayoun spent in "Hell," the five believers were sentenced to three more years in prison. Houmayoun received an additional eight months because he was on probation for previous evangelistic activities at the time of his arrest.

"LIKE THAT, THE NEW TESTAMENTS WERE SPREADING."

In total, Houmayoun was moved six times while he was in prison. He even spent a few months in solitary confinement. When the five Christians were eventually released, they were required to sign a statement that acknowledged that if they were caught joining an underground church or participating in any Christian activity, they would be imprisoned for life.

Houmayoun signed the letter with the full intent of continuing his evangelistic work anyway. Many believers who had once attended his church, however, were now reluctant to attend it out of fear that they'd be next to go to prison. After receiving repeated threats, Houmayoun and his family decided to leave Iran.

Houmayoun often thinks about inmates who heard the gospel, especially those who accepted Jesus. "Some of them are out of jail, and we are still in touch with them," he said. "Some of them have life sentences, and some are getting ready to be executed."

And Houmayoun still treasures one of his prison Bibles. "Some of the copies went to other prisons because sometimes when a prisoner was transferring to another prison, he would take copies with him to that place. There they also would make copies and, like that, the New Testaments were spreading."

No prison gates—even those in a dark prison basement known as Hell—can prevail against God's Word.

DAY 283

James 1:21–25

*Therefore put away all filthiness and rampant wickedness
and receive with meekness the implanted word, which
is able to save your souls. But be doers of the word, and
not hearers only, deceiving yourselves. For if anyone is a
hearer of the word and not a doer, he is like a man who
looks intently at his natural face in a mirror. For he looks
at himself and goes away and at once forgets what he was
like. But the one who looks into the perfect law, the law
of liberty, and perseveres, being no hearer who forgets
but a doer who acts, he will be blessed in his doing.*

Biblical disciples hunger for God's Word. By internalizing God's Word as we read it daily, we place it deep within our souls. Iranian Christians have identified 125 Scriptures they are memorizing so they'll be prepared to face certain persecution and walk in obedience to Christ. How will you remember God's Word today?

DAY 284

Psalm 33:4

For the word of the LORD is upright, and
all his work is done in faithfulness.

God's Word is upright and just; it's as pure and true as he is. So receive and share it with boldness. Let his Word fill you, flow out of you, and spill into the lives of people around you. When they ask why you're different, fearlessly tell them: It's God—all God.

> For these believers, it [the Bible] is the one thing that they cherish most because they have seen the other side and know the cost of living a life without Christ.
>
> A front-line worker in Nigeria about Christians from a Muslim background who just received a Bible

DAY 285

Luke 11:28

But he said, "Blessed rather are those who
hear the word of God and keep it!"

Biblical disciples should not pursue blessings tied to possessions or position. Godly contentment in all circumstances is a blessing that should be highly treasured. Luke reminds us that our blessing (contentment and happiness) is tied to our obedience. How are you blessed when you keep God's Word?

DAY 286

Psalm 119:9–16

*How can a young man keep his way pure? By guarding it
according to your word. With my whole heart I seek you;
let me not wander from your commandments! I have stored
up your word in my heart, that I might not sin against
you. Blessed are you, O L*ORD*; teach me your statutes! With
my lips I declare all the rules of your mouth. In the way of
your testimonies I delight as much as in all riches. I will
meditate on your precepts and fix my eyes on your ways. I
will delight in your statutes; I will not forget your word.*

In Nigeria, where 40 percent of the population is unable to read
and opposition to Christianity is fierce, audio Bibles in the tribal
languages reach people for Jesus Christ that print Bibles can't. Pray for
our Christian brothers and sisters in Nigeria who hide God's Word in
their hearts through audio Bibles. Commit to hide God's Word in your
heart—and start doing so today!

DAY 287

2 Peter 1:3–8

*His divine power has granted to us all things that pertain
to life and godliness, through the knowledge of him who
called us to his own glory and excellence, by which he has
granted to us his precious and very great promises, so that
through them you may become partakers of the divine
nature, having escaped from the corruption that is in the
world because of sinful desire. For this very reason, make
every effort to supplement your faith with virtue, and
virtue with knowledge, and knowledge with self-control,
and self-control with steadfastness, and steadfastness with
godliness, and godliness with brotherly affection, and
brotherly affection with love. For if these qualities are yours
and are increasing, they keep you from being ineffective
or unfruitful in the knowledge of our Lord Jesus Christ.*

Speak aloud the promise of God that most matters to you today. Let
it spark your obedience, faithfulness, and joy.

DAY 288

Matthew 7:24–26

"Everyone then who hears these words of mine and does them will be like a wise man who built his house on the rock. And the rain fell, and the floods came, and the winds blew and beat on that house, but it did not fall, because it had been founded on the rock. And everyone who hears these words of mine and does not do them will be like a foolish man who built his house on the sand."

Since trusting in Christ, threats and attacks are the normal daily backdrop to Aliyah's life. "I think whoever believes Jesus and serves him will suffer," she said. "We are also not just granted to believe, but to suffer." She is committed to reaching her family at great personal risk and is just as committed to sharing Jesus in her Somali community. While some might view Aliyah's behavior as reckless or even foolish, she has a different perspective. "Somebody who serves Jesus is not foolish," she insisted. "It is the best thing ever!"

DAY 289

2 Timothy 3:14–15

But as for you, continue in what you have learned and have firmly believed, knowing from whom you learned it and how from childhood you have been acquainted with the sacred writings, which are able to make you wise for salvation through faith in Christ Jesus.

Which words of God do you need to hold close as you move through today? Write them down below, meditate on them, and walk in confidence.

DAY 290

Romans 15:4

For whatever was written in former days was written for our instruction, that through endurance and through the encouragement of the Scriptures we might have hope.

After World War II, North Korea was established as an independent nation. Its leader, Kim Il Sung, outlawed all religions except the worship of himself as the "Great Leader." The government destroyed churches and confiscated Bibles. Teaching children about Jesus became dangerous and remains dangerous today. North Korean Christians receive hope when they receive a Bible, which helps them endure as Christ's followers as they obediently and carefully share the gospel despite great risk of arrest and imprisonment.

Father, as my Christian brothers and sisters in North Korea endure persecution, I ask that each one will have access to your Word so that they may find hope. Lord, may I not take the instruction of your Word for granted! Amen.

DAY 291

Proverbs 3:1–2

*My son, do not forget my teaching, but let your
heart keep my commandments, for length of days
and years of life and peace they will add to you.*

Lord, may I never forget your teachings. Engrave them on my heart
and mind so I will faithfully obey you even when fear clouds my
vision. Your commandments are wise, and your Word is honest and
true. I find my life in you, Lord. Amen.

2 Timothy 3:16–17

All Scripture is breathed out by God and profit-
able for teaching, for reproof, for correction, and
for training in righteousness, that the man of God
may be complete, equipped for every good work.

God is preparing you for action and to do good works. What are they? Ask God to reveal them to you.

It is wrong to believe the Bible because arguments prove it to be true. We do not judge the Word of God; it judges us. It is the invincible truth. Christians submit to it completely. Don't allow any spirit to separate you from any part of it.

Richard Wurmbrand

Prayer:
Our Father in Heaven

God hears from many frightened people.

When bullets sizzle past or thunderbolts crash, even people who seldom think of God quickly mutter a panicked prayer. Fear has a way of galvanizing faith—at least until the shooting stops and the tornado spirals back skyward.

And God hears those prayers because God hears all prayers that flow from sincere hearts—even sincerely frightened ones.

One night during Sabina Wurmbrand's three-year prison sentence of hard labor, her cell filled with the appalling cacophony of cries and sobs. For an hour, women relived the trauma of their interrogations. One woman after another succumbed. An evil force seemed to surround them in the foul darkness. A single bulb cast mad shadows on the vaulted ceiling.

At first, Sabina felt numb with shock. Then, like an iron that reddens in the fire, she felt something swell in her breast and found herself reliving her interrogation. Her nights were full of fear and wondering what they were doing to Richard.

She fought off madness with prayer, acting unconsciously and allowing the words to well up to God in a stream.

"As if it were the one safe place in hell, women crowded around our bunks," she wrote. "Prisoners squeezed in beside me, clasping my hands; they seemed to be fleeing from a nightmare pogrom."

The guards had experienced this tragic scene before and kept out. Soon, the sound of sobbing began to fade. In an hour, only exhausted sniffles from the dark broke the silence. The sense of fear dissolved.

"LORD,...GIVE ME ALSO WISDOM OF HEART TO WIN THEIR SOULS FOR YOU."

For a long time, Sabina lay awake, praying silently, "Lord, if you have given me some influence among these women, give me also wisdom of heart to win their souls for you."

As a Christ-follower, you have the honor of coming boldly to God. When you pray, you submit yourself to his Lordship, and you can be confident he'll respond to you according to his plan and purpose for your life.

Those things in your life that frighten you—bring them to God. Lay them out before him and acknowledge your need. Then trust that he will answer for your good and his glory.

Speak—and listen.

Share—and receive.

DAY 293

John 15:5

"I am the vine; you are the branches. Whoever
abiding in me and I in him, he it is that bears much
fruit, for apart from me you can do nothing."

You were created for connection—so stay connected. When you're abiding in Jesus, fear struggles to find a foothold in your life. Joy crowds fear out; joy and fulfillment overwhelm it. So be connected— and find life. How can you practice abiding in Christ today?

> But he who abides in him [Christ] will know deep joy, even
> in the extremes of pain.
>
> Richard Wurmbrand

DAY 294

Psalm 34:4, 6–7

*I sought the L*ORD*, and he answered me and deliv-ered me from all my fears. This poor man cried, and the L*ORD *heard him and saved him out of all his troubles. The angel of the L*ORD *encamps around those who fear him, and delivers them.*

Oh, to be delivered from fear at just the moment of your need—to live above your crisis of anxiety! That day may come as God pro-vides respite for you in your moment of angst, but it certainly comes in eternity for those who seek God. How does the certainty of that com-ing day empower the way you endure this one?

> When extreme need or threat arises, it is good to cry out. Nobody whispers when threatened by a dragon. God says to Samuel, "Their cry has come to me" (1 Samuel 9:16). If the cry is missing, the realization of our great danger in this valley is missing.
>
> Richard Wurmbrand

WHOM SHALL I FEAR?

DAY 295

Acts 16:25–26

About midnight Paul and Silas were praying and singing hymns to God, and the prisoners were listening to them, and suddenly there was a great earthquake, so that the foundations of the prison were shaken. And immediately all the doors were opened, and everyone's bonds were unfastened.

Why sing at midnight? Perhaps because that's when fears, like prison rats, came nibbling at Paul and Silas. The night is often the time when our fears surface. The next time that happens to you, pray aloud and declare God's Word in song. Watch your fears slink away.

I remembered a passage in Richard Wurmbrand's book, *Tortured for Christ*, about how Christians, like nightingales, could not be prevented from singing even in captivity, and I suggested that we sing: "We should praise God in spite of the fleas, in spite of the lice, in spite of the heat. We should thank God despite our circumstances." So I began to sing with them, and pray, and share the Word of God from memory.

Helen Berhane, while in prison in Eritrea for her faith

DAY 296

Psalm 50:14–15

*Offer to God a sacrifice of thanksgiving, and perform
your vows to the Most High, and call upon me in the day
of trouble; I will deliver you, and you shall glorify me.*

When trouble thunders into your life, call out to God. Ask him for deliverance and know that he's worthy of your thanks and praise no matter how—or when—he responds. Lean on him always in days of pain, fear, isolation, and joy. Write your prayer to God below.

DAY 297

John 15:26–27

"But when the Helper comes, whom I will send to you from the Father, the Spirit of truth, who proceeds from the Father, he will bear witness about me. And you also will bear witness, because you have been with me from the beginning."

Rocio was known for sharing the gospel with everyone she met, especially the guerrilla fighters in Colombia's dangerous "red zones." "All who come here will hear about Christ," she said. Rocio and her husband, James, had already gone to bed one night when they heard an unexpected knock at the front door.

"Is your name Maria?" the man asked her.

"No, I am Rocio Pino," she replied.

Three gunshots shattered the stillness of the night, and when James turned around, he saw his wife fall to the ground.

Knowing the risks of where they lived, Rocio and her husband chose to bear witness to the salvation that can be found only through faith in Christ.

DAY 298

Psalm 55:22

Cast your burden on the LORD, and he will sustain you; he will never permit the righteous to be moved.

What burdens weigh you down that you are finally ready to give to God? Why have you held onto them for so long? Write a prayer of surrender to him below. Thank your Heavenly Father that in the face of your anxiety, he is able!

_____

_____

_____

_____

_____

_____

DAY 299

Hebrews 7:22, 25–26

This makes Jesus the guarantor of a better covenant.
Consequently, he is able to save to the uttermost those who
draw near to God through him, since he always lives to
make intercession for them. For it was indeed fitting that we
should have such a high priest, holy, innocent, unstained,
separated from sinners, and exalted above the heavens.

Jesus, you intercede for me. I couldn't have a better advocate and a more faithful friend to stand before God and speak on my behalf. I am utterly unworthy of this, Jesus; I know I'm a recipient of your gracious love. Thank you! Thank you! Amen.

DAY 300

Psalm 62:7–8

On God rests my salvation and my glory; my mighty rock,
my refuge is God. Trust in him at all times, O people;
pour out your heart before him; God is a refuge for us.

Y ou know this religion is the foreigner's religion," government officials told Keo. "It is not your Lao religion." Keo and his wife
refused to sign a document that indicated they had renounced their
faith. After they witnessed God's power in the healing of their son,
how could they deny him? Keo said his relatives were slowly accept-
ing the truth of Christ but were fearful of the persecution they could
face if they decided to trust Christ. Keo assured them that the God of
the Bible would be with them. Keo and his wife saw God at work in
people's lives as they actively shared the gospel. Their home is now a
house church. Keo continues to place his trust in the Lord and knows
his future is in God's hands.

How can you emulate his example today?

DAY 301

Romans 12:12

*Rejoice in hope, be patient in tribula-
tion, be constant in prayer.*

Three tough assignments—but each brings grace that lets you live beyond the instability of emotions that stem from your circumstances. Joy, patience, and prayer unlock shackles of fear and invite you into the arms of the God who loves you. So choose to rejoice. Decide to be patient. And celebrate God's constant presence in your life.

DAY 302

Philippians 4:6–7

Do not be anxious about anything, but in everything by prayer and supplication with thanksgiving let your requests be made known to God. And the peace of God, which surpasses all understanding, will guard your hearts and your minds in Christ Jesus.

Three Indian Christians were arrested for sharing the gospel. While they were in custody, one of the men's wives wrote: "I am feeling at peace knowing God is in control of this situation. I am asking that he would be glorified and the national believers to be encouraged and their faith strengthened. I am starting to feel tired and drained, but still hopeful in him and all the ways he desires to use this and be glorified." The men were later released.

Pray today about what's causing you anxiety and uncertainty. But rather than simply telling God about the circumstances that concern you, wrap them in trust and hand them over to God. Ask in return that God's unexplainable peace would flood your life as it flooded this Christian sister's life in India. Then watch what happens in the coming days as God works in and through you.

DAY 303

Psalm 64:1–3, 10

*Hear my voice, O God, in my complaint; preserve my life
from dread of the enemy. Hide me from the secret plots
of the wicked, from the throng of evildoers, who whet
their tongues like swords, who aim bitter words like
arrows. Let the righteous one rejoice in the Lord and take
refuge in him! Let all the upright in heart exult!*

Richard Wurmbrand stood before a gathering that attempted to
sway Romania's pastors to accept atheistic Communist teaching
and assimilate it within the church. Despite the obvious repercussions,
Richard stood—at Sabina's prompting—and spoke boldly against those
who held his life in their hands. The prayer of Richard's life was to be
found faithful, at any cost, and he acted courageously upon that prayer.

What does bold faith look like in your life today?

Praying for a Changed Heart

Once a month, Tavesa invites six women to her small, dilapidated home in Nepal. The women read Scripture and pray, ignoring the idols and pictures of Hindu gods peering blindly at them from nearby tables and surrounding walls.

When Tavesa's husband died, her twenty-four-year-old son took over her home and forced her to move into his run-down house. As a zealous Hindu, he ruled his widowed mother like a dictator and insisted she leave the idols and pictures of his favorite gods where he placed them.

"The only thing that I can do is pray and ask God to change his heart," Tavesa said. "If I take the photos down, he would probably beat me."

Tavesa became a Christian two years after her husband died when she received healing through the prayers of a Christian in her village. Losing her husband and embracing faith in Christ cost her dearly.

As a widow, Tavesa was considered cursed, and she had no status. In Nepal's Hindu culture, property owned by a late husband goes to the children, usually the oldest son. For at least the first year following a husband's death, widows must wear white. And many people avoid Nepal's roughly half a million widows in public because they believe the widow's bad luck could be transferred to them.

When Tavesa declared her faith in Christ, her adult son and two daughters viewed her as worthless. Her son continued to force his Hindu beliefs on her. Each year during an annual Hindu festival, he hung a poster of snakes on her front door. In Hindu mythology, snakes represent mortality, death, and rebirth. Worshipers offer gifts like incense and fruit to snake idols, hoping to gain knowledge and wealth.

Tavesa said the snake festivals test her faith, especially the first one she experienced as a Christian. Her children wanted her to celebrate with them and perform the Hindu act of worship called puja by offering flowers and fruit to the idols and snakes. "Even then, I had decided to follow Christ and not turn back, no matter what my children say," she said. "Jesus gave me a new life, so this life is for him."

> "THE ONLY THING THAT I CAN DO IS PRAY..."

Tavesa prays her children will also come to know the one true God. "My major prayer request now is for my children," she said, "I have lost my husband without him knowing Christ. I don't want that to happen to my children."

Tavesa's son believes he's honoring his father by working to ensure that his family remains Hindu. And Tavesa can't challenge him because he's now head of the family. The boldest act she's taken—other than publicly professing faith in Christ—was to hang a cross on her wall. But one of her daughters took it down. She believed the cross would anger the Hindu gods.

Still, through Tavesa's persistent prayers to the one true God, she's seen hopeful signs that her son's heart is softening. He now allows her to attend church services in the city, although he doesn't pay for her bus fare as he does when she travels there for other reasons. Tavesa is grateful to God that she's now able to worship with other Christians.

And more recently, her son began to allow the monthly prayer meetings in her home. Since Tavesa never attended school, church members are helping her learn how to read the Bible that their pastor gave to her. She said she's especially moved by verses about the protection and care of widows, and she also enjoys the Psalms which encourage her during times of spiritual isolation at home.

One particular verse she found helpful is Matthew 5:44, in which Jesus tells us to love our enemies and pray for those who persecute us. "From the time I first read that," she said, "I am praying for them also because they are not persecuting me, but they are persecuting Jesus. I realize whatever people tell me, they are not telling it to me but to Jesus. From that time, I am praying for the people around me and my children."

Although Tavesa lives alone, she knows God is with her. "I am alone nowhere," she said. "Jesus is with me and there are so many people praying for me, so I am not alone."

DAY 304

Philippians 1:19–20, 29

For I know that through your prayers and the help of the Spirit of Jesus Christ this will turn out for my deliverance, as it is my eager expectation and hope that I will not be at all ashamed, but that with full courage now as always Christ will be honored in my body, whether by life or by death. For it has been granted to you that for the sake of Christ you should not only believe in him but also suffer for his sake.

From shame to boldness. From fear to courage. Intercessory prayer, praying on behalf of someone else, is a spark that ignites strength in the hearts of those who are weary. Pray for someone today who's hurting and who needs deep healing.

DAY 305

Psalm 118:5-7

Out of my distress I called on the LORD; the LORD answered me and set me free. The LORD is on my side; I will not fear. What can man do to me? The LORD is on my side as my helper; I shall look in triumph on those who hate me.

When Hussein, an Iranian Christian who had converted from Islam, began to boldly share the gospel with others, he was arrested, blindfolded, and led to jail. Weary and afraid, his mind turned to Jesus. As he began to pray, God's presence filled his solitary cell. Hussein said, "I was in the presence of Jesus, and I was praying more boldly and confidently that Jesus had brought me there for a purpose."

How will you turn to prayer today as you face a difficult circumstance?

DAY 306

1 Peter 5:4, 6–7

*And when the chief Shepherd appears, you will receive
the unfading crown of glory. Humble yourselves,
therefore, under the mighty hand of God so that at
the proper time he may exalt you, casting all your
anxieties on him, because he cares for you.*

We may often hold something back when we come to God.
Today, tell him the last one percent, that last thing you've not
admitted to anyone, perhaps even to yourself. Humble yourself and
cast your fears and anxiety on him—all of them. He can handle it, for
he cares for you.

DAY 307

Proverbs 1:33

But whoever listens to me will dwell secure and
will be at ease, without dread of disaster.

Pause and picture yourself holding your fear, insecurity, and doubt in your hand. Now lift that hand to God and release what you hold. What does God say in response to your action? What comforting words does he have for you? Write them down below and thank him.

DAY 308

Acts 18:9–10

And the Lord said to Paul one night in a vision, "Do not be afraid, but go on speaking and do not be silent, for I am with you, and no one will attack you to harm you, for I have many in this city who are my people."

Prayer is not only speaking to God but listening to what he has to say. Spend a quiet moment today, and listen to the Lord's instruction that will lift you above every fear you face.

> If you say that men with reason and knowledge do not believe in God, why do you fear when I, an ignorant, speak with reasonable men? Why do you put me in prison? Even our ancestors of thousands of years ago did not do this, those about whom you say that they were so primitive as to invent a heaven and a hell because they could not understand the laws of nature and society.
>
> Aida Skripnikova, imprisoned in the Soviet Union for her Christian witness, to her judges

DAY 309

Isaiah 58:9–11

"Then you shall call, and the Lord *will answer; you shall cry, and he will say, 'Here I am.' If you take away the yoke from your midst, the pointing of the finger, and speaking wickedness, if you pour yourself out for the hungry and satisfy the desire of the afflicted, then shall your light rise in the darkness and your gloom be as the noonday. And the* Lord *will guide you continually and satisfy your desire in scorched places and make your bones strong; and you shall be like a watered garden, like a spring of water, whose waters do not fail."*

Is there anything more reassuring than to call out in the dark and hear someone who loves you respond, "I'm here"? Well, God is there. In whatever circumstance darkness has hold of you, he's there. Call out—and find comfort.

> We pray that we depend on God when we lack because apart from him we have no good thing.
>
> Elder Li, a Christian who was detained in China

DAY 310

Lamentations 3:57–58

You came near when I called on you; you said,
"Do not fear!" You have taken up my cause,
O Lord; you have redeemed my life.

The Lord's proximity to us begins with a prayer. When you call
on God—when you pray—God draws near; his love for you is
larger than your fear. He then takes up your cause and redeems your
situation. So tell God what you fear. Ask him to redeem it—and you.
Write your prayer below.

DAY 311

1 John 5:14–15

*And this is the confidence that we have toward him, that
if we ask anything according to his will he hears us. And
if we know that he hears us in whatever we ask, we know
that we have the requests that we have asked of him.*

God is listening. Confidently ask him for what you need—do it
now. Then thank him for hearing your prayers.

WHOM SHALL I FEAR?

DAY 312

Daniel 10:12

Then he said to me, "Fear not, Daniel, for from the first day that you set your heart to understand and humbled yourself before your God, your words have been heard, and I have come because of your words."

P rayers from humble hearts are well received. Would people who know you well say you're humble? Would God say that of you? Ask him to show you if you are humble.

DAY 313

Ephesians 3:11–12, 14, 16–19

This was according to the eternal purpose that he has realized in Christ Jesus our Lord, in whom we have boldness and access with confidence through our faith in him. For this reason I bow my knees before the Father, that according to the riches of his glory he may grant you to be strengthened with power through his Spirit in your inner being, so that Christ may dwell in your hearts through faith—that you, being rooted and grounded in love, may have strength to comprehend with all the saints what is the breadth and length and height and depth, and to know the love of Christ that surpasses knowledge, that you may be filled with all the fullness of God.

Paul wrote these words while in prison. Imagine what that must have been like—chains chafing his ankles, hunger gnawing at his gut, isolated and alone. How does Paul urging you to know the love of Christ inspire you to live out your faith today boldly, fearlessly, joyfully?

DAY 314

1 Chronicles 16:11–12

Seek the LORD and his strength; seek his presence continually! Remember the wondrous works that he has done, his miracles and the judgments he uttered.

Nadia, an Iranian Christian, was concerned about her roommate who had been involved in occult and voodoo practices and experienced anxiety and feelings of hopelessness. Two ladies agreed to visit Nadia and pray with her in her apartment. After they arrived, Nadia's roommate joined them. As they talked and prayed, her roommate wanted to know more about Jesus Christ because her feelings of anxiety and depression had lifted. The believers shared how praying to Christ had helped them. Later, Nadia's roommate told her that she slept better that night than she had in a long time. Since then, the roommates have studied Scripture together.

If you're seeking God, you'll find him. God shines in every Scriptural account of his wondrous works, his powerful miracles, and his encounters with people like Nadia, her roommate, and you. Reach out to Jesus from the place of your fear. Remember what he has done for you.

Lifted From Despair

After Domiana's husband died, she sank into deep despair. Her husband's parents, who were no longer willing to support Domiana and her children, took the family's belongings and kicked them out of their home.

Domiana lived in a poor neighborhood in Egypt and raised three preteens on her own without any income. She struggled to survive. She received no support from the local Islamic community and, to make matters worse, she battled a chronic illness.

After multiple treatments failed to improve her condition, she faced the difficult decision of whether to undergo a risky operation. "I had to do many surgeries to remove cysts," she said, "and it didn't work. The doctor said it would be dangerous to do another operation."

But the physician, who was a Christian, advised one additional treatment—prayer. "The doctor told me that Jesus can heal," she recalled, "and [that I should] ask the real God for a breakthrough." Her cysts disappeared days later without a trace of the disease remaining.

After experiencing this miracle through prayer, Domiana felt abandoned by the religion she'd followed since childhood, so she cried out to the One True God to reveal himself to her. "I asked God to enlighten my path," she said. "I told him I'm astray."

As Domiana continued to seek God, she experienced a vision of Christ speaking to her. Though fearful and confused, she felt immediate peace. She wanted the same peace for her children, so she asked Jesus to reveal himself to them so they could know him, too.

The children noticed an immediate difference in their mother as well as a new peace that pervaded their home. After Domiana shared the news of her healing with them, they wanted to know more about Jesus and how he'd transformed her. Soon, all of her children placed their faith in Christ, and the family began to attend a church in Cairo.

> "I ASKED GOD TO ENLIGHTEN MY PATH."

While Domiana had found physical healing and her family had found peace in Christ, her journey of suffering was far from over. Within a few weeks, the news spread that Domiana and her children had left Islam to follow Christ. Local Muslims who saw her leave the church followed her home. After they saw a pastor visit her house with Bibles, they broke in and physically assaulted her and the pastor. They eventually set the building on fire and also burned several churches in the area to stop others from turning to Christ.

"Many people invaded our house and kicked us out of our apartment," Domiana said. "We spent three days on the street. I was frightened and sad about my kids being cold in the street, but at the same time, I was secure in my heart and knew that we were following the truth."

After they moved to another apartment, Domiana and her children immediately faced more opposition and threats from

Islamic religious leaders. Eventually, the threats turned to violence. Local Muslims broke into the family's new apartment and tortured Domiana's son. They cut a tattoo off his arm that identified him as a Christian. They also threatened to kill Domiana and her children unless they returned to Islam, but Domiana stood firm in her faith. "I was confident that God would take care of us," she said.

After the attack, the Muslims who broke into the family's apartment watched them closely and prevented them from leaving even to get food. Trapped and isolated, Domiana sought help from the Lord. "I prayed, 'If you want to use us, you let us out,'" she said.

After they finally escaped, Domiana and her children were suddenly on the run. An Egyptian pastor became aware of Domiana's situation and helped the family relocate to a neighboring country. Though Domiana faced many challenges, her faith has never wavered, and she hopes that God will use her story for his purposes.

"Every day is better than yesterday," she said. "The Lord has been faithful to me. He has not left us. I only ask God to use us for his glory."

DAY 315

Daniel 10:19

And he said, "O man greatly loved, fear not, peace be with you; be strong and of good courage." And as he spoke to me, I was strengthened and said, "Let my lord speak, for you have strengthened me."

Daniel lived faithfully for many years under the rule and reign of the Babylonian king. He was in a season of discouragement and weariness when God's angel spoke these refreshing words to him. God's words of encouragement must have strengthened Daniel in a dark and dangerous time. Write out some promises from God that have encouraged you during times of difficulty. Let them send your fears running; those fears are no match for the courage God can ignite in your heart.

DAY 316

Micah 7:7

*But as for me, I will look to the LORD; I will wait for
the God of my salvation; my God will hear me.*

Waiting is hard, yet the truth is that God's timeline is better than
our own. In waiting, our trust for him grows. Our dependence
on him deepens. We find our true place in life, surrendered to God,
and become willing to serve him no matter what and no matter when.

WHOM SHALL I FEAR?

DAY 317

John 16:13

*"When the Spirit of truth comes, he will guide you
into all the truth, for he will not speak on his own
authority, but whatever he hears he will speak, and
he will declare to you the things that are to come."*

Lord, how good you are! You've sent a guide and called me to listen and obediently follow. But I sometimes struggle with both listening and obedience, Lord. Forgive me. Sharpen my hearing and soften my heart. Lead me to a place of joyful submission to you. That's where I'll find peace. That's where hope lives. Amen.

DAY 318

Acts 12:5

So Peter was kept in prison, but earnest prayer
for him was made to God by the church.

Without a trial, Twen was imprisoned in Eritrea for her active faith. She endured terrible beatings and torture at the hands of Eritrean prison guards. On occasion, Twen took the punishment of her ill cellmate. The global body of Christ united in prayer for Twen's release, and God answered those prayers when Twen was released after more than 14 years of imprisonment.

Thank you, Father, that the global body of Christ is united in earnest prayer one for another. Amen.

DAY 319

1 Thessalonians 5:16–18

*Rejoice always, pray without ceasing, give
thanks in all circumstances; for this is the
will of God in Christ Jesus for you.*

Give thanks in all circumstances? That's easy to say but harder to do. So when you're pressed down, cornered, and the spotlight of discovery swings toward something you desperately wish stayed hidden, don't cower. Give thanks. Ask God what he wants you to learn and how you can lean more fully on him.

> There was once a fiddler who played so beautifully that everybody danced. A deaf man who could not hear the music considered them all mad. Those who are with Jesus in suffering hear this music to which other men are deaf. They dance and do not care if they are considered insane. Other men could not understand the joy of the suffering Christians, just as a frog in a well could not understand the mighty ocean.
>
> Richard Wurmbrand

DAY 320

Hebrews 4:14–16

Since then we have a great high priest who has passed through the heavens, Jesus, the Son of God, let us hold fast our confession. For we do not have a high priest who is unable to sympathize with our weaknesses, but one who in every respect has been tempted as we are, yet without sin. Let us then with confidence draw near to the throne of grace, that we may receive mercy and find grace to help in time of need.

Jesus sympathizes with your weaknesses. How does knowing you'll find mercy and understanding give you the confidence to pray today?

DAY 321

Job 3:24–26

*For my sighing comes instead of my bread, and my groanings
are poured out like water. For the thing that I fear comes
upon me, and what I dread befalls me. I am not at ease,
nor am I quiet; I have no rest, but trouble comes.*

Those things we fear that sometimes come to pass—sickness, the
death of a loved one—can be sudden losses that send us into a
tailspin. In those moments, choose to focus on God, not your troubles.
Jesus Christ can give you strength to cope and the hope that sustains
you.

DAY 322

James 1:5–6

*If any of you lacks wisdom, let him ask God, who
gives generously to all without reproach, and it will
be given him. But let him ask in faith, with no
doubting, for the one who doubts is like a wave of
the sea that is driven and tossed by the wind.*

Don't let fear and negative emotions paralyze you from asking God
for wisdom. He's inviting you to ask; he's eager to provide it.
His wisdom will deliver you from the winds and waves. It will place
your feet back on solid ground when everything else is shifting around
you. List those fears and negative emotions below, followed by a prayer
asking God for wisdom as you navigate your way through difficult
circumstances.

DAY 323

2 Kings 6:14–17

*So he sent there horses and chariots and a great army, and they came by night and surrounded the city. When the servant of the man of God rose early in the morning and went out, behold, an army with horses and chariots was all around the city. And the servant said, "Alas, my master! What shall we do?" He said, "Do not be afraid, for those who are with us are more than those who are with them." Then Elisha prayed and said, "O L*ORD*, please open his eyes that he may see." So the Lord opened the eyes of the young man, and he saw, and behold, the mountain was full of horses and chariots of fire all around Elisha.*

DAY 324

1 John 1:9

*If we confess our sins, he is faithful and just to forgive
us our sins and to cleanse us from all unrighteousness.*

Your prayers become real the moment you begin to confess. Confession clears away posturing and lays bare who you are—who you really are. And it opens you to receive God's loving, cleansing touch. Washed clean, you're free to walk in boldness, to sleep in peace. What do you need to confess to him today? Write your confession below.

DAY 325

Jeremiah 29:12–14

Then you will call upon me and come and pray to me, and I will hear you. You will seek me and find me, when you seek me with all your heart. I will be found by you, declares the L ORD, and I will restore your fortunes and gather you from all the nations and all the places where I have driven you, declares the L ORD, and I will bring you back to the place from which I sent you into exile.

If your circumstances are such that you feel in exile, don't be dismayed. God hasn't lost sight of you. Tell him how you feel and ask that he draw you back from your place of pain.

DAY 326

Matthew 7:7–11

"Ask, and it will be given to you; seek, and you will find; knock, and it will be opened to you. For everyone who asks receives, and the one who seeks finds, and to the one who knocks it will be opened. Or which one of you, if his son asks him for bread, will give him a stone? Or if he asks for a fish, will give him a serpent? If you then, who are evil, know how to give good gifts to your children, how much more will your Father who is in heaven give good things to those who ask him!"

Lord, you are the giver of all that's good, all that's true, all that's holy and pure. Thank you for such gifts! Thank you for your saving grace, your tender mercy, and your steadfast love that isn't held back from me. You generously pour out your love on me. You are holy, Lord—and I am wholly yours. Amen.

God's Faithfulness:
Our Antidote to Fear

When we trust God, we move forward even though we're unsure of what may lie around the next corner. All we know—all we need to know as we go where God directs—is that we're not walking alone.

Our faithful God walks with us. No matter what's around the corner, he won't forsake or forget us. No matter when we call on him, he's faithful to hear us and respond.

Faithfulness is a defining characteristic of God—it's who he is and always will be. His steady love for you doesn't depend on whether you remembered to pray this morning or didn't flee temptation this afternoon. He's not going anywhere—and his arms are always wide to invite you home, should you wander away.

God's faithfulness is an antidote to fear. He always keeps his promises—and he's made promises to you.

He's promised that nothing can shake you from his hands and heart.

He's promised that through the sacrifice of Christ, your sins are forgiven.

He's promised to make a place for you in heaven.

He's promised to be with you now—and forever.

Many promises are made that aren't kept, but God stands alone in this: he has never made a promise he has not kept. His faithfulness is iron-clad. You can count on him—always. Throughout history, Christians who faced death because of their faith in Christ bear witness to God's faithfulness.

"HOW CAN I BLASPHEME MY KING WHO SAVED ME?"

Polycarp, the bishop of Smyrna in the second century, knew his life was in danger. A group of Christians had just been executed in the arena on account of their faith. Still, he refused to leave Rome. The Roman proconsul searched for him for days. They finally learned where he was staying, and soldiers entered the house to arrest him. But instead of fleeing, Polycarp calmly said, "God's will be done." He then asked his hosts to bring food for the soldiers and requested an hour for prayer before they arrested him. Amazed by an 86-year-old's fearlessness, the Roman soldiers granted his request.

After the soldiers brought Polycarp to the stadium, the Roman proconsul gave him a final chance to live. All Polycarp had to do was swear by Caesar and say, "Take away the atheists," as the Roman Empire called Christians for refusing to worship the Roman gods.

Polycarp looked at the roaring crowd and proclaimed, "Take away the atheists!"

The proconsul continued, "Swear, and I will let you go. Reproach Christ!"

Polycarp turned to the proconsul and boldly declared these words that reflected God's faithfulness: "Eighty-six years I have served him, and he has done me no wrong. How can I blaspheme my King who saved me?"

The proconsul urged Polycarp again and even threatened to throw him to wild beasts if he did not recant.

Still, Polycarp's faith in Jesus Christ was unmoved. And his death was certain.

Polycarp was taken to the marketplace where they prepared the pyre. Polycarp prayed as the soldiers arranged the wood. They lit the pyre, but Polycarp remained untouched by the fire. In the end, the proconsul commanded an executioner to stab him. A great quantity of his blood put out the remaining fire, and Polycarp bled to death.

Be inspired by Polycarp's example. He faced death and lived in freedom, not fear. Trust God. He is a faithful Father.

DAY 327

Genesis 26:24

*And the L*ORD *appeared to him the same night and said, "I am the God of Abraham your father. Fear not, for I am with you and will bless you and multiply your offspring for my servant Abraham's sake."*

Like us, Abraham walked in obedience and stumbled in failure, yet God remained faithful to his promise. What was true for Abraham is true for you too. God is always faithful. What he says, he means. What he promises, he'll deliver. How has God's faithfulness been evident in your life? Use the space below to write about it, and then thank him.

DAY 328

2 Thessalonians 3:1–5

*Finally, brothers, pray for us, that the word of the Lord may
speed ahead and be honored, as happened among you, and
that we may be delivered from wicked and evil men. For not
all have faith. But the Lord is faithful. He will establish you
and guard you against the evil one. And we have confidence
in the Lord about you, that you are doing and will do the
things that we command. May the Lord direct your hearts
to the love of God and to the steadfastness of Christ.*

Paul asked for prayer that God would deliver him from wicked,
evil men. Our persecuted brothers and sisters in Christ ask the
same, so pray for them today. And praise God for establishing them
and guarding them against the evil one.

DAY 329

Deuteronomy 4:37–40

And because he loved your fathers and chose their off-spring after them and brought you out of Egypt with his own presence, by his great power, driving out before you nations greater and mightier than you, to bring you in, to give you their land for an inheritance, as it is this day, know therefore today, and lay it to your heart, that the Lord is God in heaven above and on the earth beneath; there is no other. Therefore you shall keep his statutes and his commandments, which I command you today, that it may go well with you and with your children after you, and that you may prolong your days in the land that the Lord your God is giving you for all time.

Lord, it's true: you're faithful to the core. I know this to be true because of Christ. In him, though I sin, you don't reject me. I fail, and you don't scold me. Thank you for your patient, persistent, and everlasting love. Amen.

DAY 330

Hebrews 13:5–6

*Keep your life free from love of money, and be content
with what you have, for he has said, "I will never leave
you nor forsake you." So we can confidently say, "The Lord
is my helper; I will not fear; what can man do to me?"*

Few things in life qualify for the word "never." This is a world of compromise, half-truths, and forgotten promises. Only God is forever faithful. He will never leave you or forsake you—never. So what do you have to fear?

DAY 331

Jeremiah 31:1–3

*"At that time, declares the L*ORD*, I will be the God of all the clans of Israel, and they shall be my people." Thus says the L*ORD*: "The people who survived the sword found grace in the wilderness; when Israel sought for rest, the L*ORD *appeared to him from far away. I have loved you with an everlasting love; therefore I have continued my faithfulness to you."*

Lord, I'm amazed by your everlasting love. Everlasting! How wonderful to be loved so deeply, to be loved without end. I know it's true, but help me experience it deep in my bones. May my confidence in your love become complete, the bedrock of my life, the shelter I run to when fear gnaws at me. How can I be troubled when you love me now and forever? How can I do anything but love and obey you? Amen.

DAY 332

2 Corinthians 5:1

*For we know that if the tent that is our earthly home
is destroyed, we have a building from God, a house
not made with hands, eternal in the heavens.*

By many standards, the possessions of Sudanese families in the
Nuba Mountains would be considered scant and primitive. Their
homes, grass-roofed tukels (round huts made of mud with thatched
roofs), contain almost nothing of value. But these brothers and sisters
are willing to make great sacrifices for what they will possess in heaven,
not earthly possessions. Someday, they will experience the promise of
this verse, that they "have a building from God...eternal in the heavens." The price that Sudanese Christians pay is very high, but their
reward will be great. It is this eternal possession that gives them the
courage to withstand brutal assaults on their faith.

DAY 333

Psalm 56:3–4, 8–9

*When I am afraid, I put my trust in you. In God,
whose word I praise, in God I trust; I shall not be
afraid. What can flesh do to me? You have kept count
of my tossings; put my tears in your bottle. Are they not
in your book? Then my enemies will turn back in the
day when I call. This I know, that God is for me.*

Let this truth sink in for a moment: God is for you. Repeat those words when you fear that you're alone or unloved, friendless or forgotten. God is for you. He knows your troubles and tracks your tears. And he faithfully stands with you. No matter what—God is for you.

DAY 334

Isaiah 40:29–31

He gives power to the faint, and to him who has no might he increases strength. Even youths shall faint and be weary, and young men shall fall exhausted; but they who wait for the LORD shall renew their strength; they shall mount up with wings like eagles; they shall run and not be weary; they shall walk and not faint.

What do you feel today? Joy? Worry? Fear? Isolation? Some days you soar, some days you run, and other days you struggle to stand. No matter what this day brings you, thank God for his faithfulness. He is with you. He loves you. And in time, he will lift you above anything you fear. Run without becoming weary, and walk without fainting.

DAY 335

Matthew 19:26–28

But Jesus looked at them and said, "With man this is impossible, but with God all things are possible." Then Peter said in reply, "See, we have left everything and followed you. What then will we have?" Jesus said to them, "Truly, I say to you, in the new world, when the Son of Man will sit on his glorious throne, you who have followed me will also sit on twelve thrones, judging the twelve tribes of Israel."

Jesus' disciples left everything to follow him. They trusted that Jesus Christ was better than anything they left behind. Our persecuted brothers and sisters do the same. Driven from their homes, many have only the clothes they're wearing. Yet these persecuted brothers and sisters remain firm in Christ because they know life in him is superior to everything else. What has God called you to leave behind in obedience to Christ? What fears and insecurities do you need to release in light of God's love for you?

DAY 336

Psalm 31:23–24

Love the LORD, all you his saints! The LORD preserves the faithful but abundantly repays the one who acts in pride. Be strong, and let your heart take courage, all you who wait for the LORD!

Since Abdullah of Bangladesh placed his trust in Christ, his family had tried very hard to change his mind. They talked to Abdullah and tried to convince him to return to Islam. When that didn't work, they beat him. Then they called others in to beat him more severely. His mother tried to starve him and put only ashes on his plate. Abdullah prayed for God's strength, and he stood strong. As a last resort, the family called on the mullah (an Islamic religious leader) to rid the boy of the "devil." The mullah recited Islamic prayers over Abdullah. He chanted. He danced and yelled. After five hours, the mullah gave up, exhausted. Abdullah refused to turn away from Christ. A few short months later, he had led twenty-seven Muslims to faith in Christ!

Take courage today and wait upon the Lord—he is faithful!

DAY 337

Romans 8:1–2, 18, 24–25

*There is therefore now no condemnation for those who
are in Christ Jesus. For the law of the Spirit of life has set
you free in Christ Jesus from the law of sin and death. For
I consider that the sufferings of this present time are not
worth comparing with the glory that is to be revealed to
us. For in this hope we were saved. Now hope that is seen
is not hope. For who hopes for what he sees? But if we hope
for what we do not see, we wait for it with patience.*

God, your grace unshackles me from sin and unchains me from
death. You shatter the prison of my fear, and I lift my heart to
you in gratitude. I declare to all who will listen: you alone are life.
You alone are freedom. How fierce your love, God, how tender your
mercies! Amen.

DAY 338

Psalm 46:1–2

God is our refuge and strength, a very present help in trou-
ble. Therefore we will not fear though the earth gives way,
though the mountains be moved into the heart of the sea.

The psalmist wrote that God is "a very present help"—not a past help or a future help, but a present help. That is right now. Where do you need God's help today—right now? Tell him exactly what you need and look expectantly for his faithful response.

DAY 339

Isaiah 54:4–6, 10

*"Fear not, for you will not be ashamed; be not confounded,
for you will not be disgraced; for you will forget the
shame of your youth, and the reproach of your widow-
hood you will remember no more. For your Maker is your
husband, the Lord of hosts is his name; and the Holy One
of Israel is your Redeemer, the God of the whole earth he
is called. For the Lord has called you like a wife deserted
and grieved in spirit, like a wife of youth when she is
cast off, says your God. For the mountains may depart
and the hills be removed, but my steadfast love shall not
depart from you, and my covenant of peace shall not be
removed," says the Lord, who has compassion on you.*

God's faithfulness comes paired with his relentless compassion.
His tenderness enfolds those who are weak, and those who feel
disgraced or alone. He turns their eyes from their loss and failure to
himself. God replaces their despair with hope. That is your Lord. That
is your God. Praise him!

When Terror Comes Home

Throughout their marriage, Faizah watched her husband, Nagawo, faithfully serve Christians in Ethiopia. As the outreach coordinator for the local district of a large denomination, Nagawo encouraged believers to reach out to their Muslim neighbors. Faizah and Nagawo had once been Muslims. But for the past three decades, they'd worked to reach Muslims with the gospel and help new believers mature in their faith.

One night, Faizah was at home with her daughter and granddaughter, waiting for Nagawo to return from his ministry work. Suddenly, several houses nearby went up in flames. Faizah said the attack was so sudden and violent that it "erupted like thunder." Soon 16 houses collapsed in flames, which continued to spread to neighboring homes.

When the mob of Islamists igniting the fires approached her house, Faizah and her family had nowhere to run. "Lord, if my soul is yours, deliver us from this!" Faizah cried out.

The men dragged Faizah and her family outside. They watched in horror as the attackers doused their home with gasoline and set it ablaze. "Lord, if this fire is from you," Faizah prayed, "let it continue; no one can stop it. But if this fire is from the devil, let it be extinguished."

Shortly after she prayed, a sudden rain extinguished the fire. Although half of her home continued to smolder and smoke, Faizah was grateful that the fire didn't consume everything.

But the frustrated mob began to steal her food and other belongings. They destroyed whatever remained in Faizah's home. Then Faizah heard a frightening shout from a celebrating Islamist: "We killed the main person! The leader is dead!"

As the attackers sang with joy, Faizah's heart sank. She followed the crowd until her worst fears were confirmed. She saw Nagawo's beheaded body lying on the ground. The men who killed him danced around his body as Faizah wept in horror. Faizah and her daughter ran to Nagawo, picked up his head, and dragged his body away from the attackers. With their home partly destroyed and nowhere to take Nagawo's body, they covered it up and sat beside it, weeping, until help arrived in the morning.

"HE HAS HELPED ME TO PASS THROUGH THESE DIFFICULTIES."

Faizah later learned the Islamists had killed her husband because he, a former Muslim, had led many others to leave Islam and place their faith in Christ. When asked how the loss of her husband, her home, and all of her belongings affected her faith, Faizah said, "Even while the flames were shooting up, I was thanking God. And even when I saw that my husband had died, I maintained my relationship with Jesus. For the past thirty years, I have been intimately serving Jesus. He has helped me to pass through these difficulties, and I believe that he will help me even more."

Faizah said that with the Holy Spirit's help, she forgave those who attacked her family and brutally murdered her husband. "When I saw that person who took the knife and beheaded my husband," she said, "as a Christian, I'm not going to do something against him. I forgive, but I don't forget."

"As I lost my beloved husband, we are now separated as human beings, and I feel sad about that," she said. "But he has gone to a better place, and I'm encouraged about that. And I'm thankful that God spared me and my daughter."

Faizah wants to continue to reach out to Muslims with the gospel. "Even though I lost my husband," she explained, "when I saw [the Muslims'] lives and how they live, I know that I'm living in the right way. I want them to come to Christ."

Faizah encourages other Christian widows whose husbands were persecuted to keep their eyes on Jesus. "God has comforted me when I lost my husband; God has blessed me," she said. "So please, trust in him and be encouraged in Christ."

And Faizah is continuing the work she and her husband began three decades ago—sharing the gospel with her Muslim neighbors.

DAY 340

Jeremiah 17:7–8

Blessed is the man who trusts in the LORD, whose trust is the LORD. He is like a tree planted by water, that sends out its roots by the stream, and does not fear when heat comes, for its leaves remain green, and is not anxious in the year of drought, for it does not cease to bear fruit.

Have you ever encountered times of spiritual drought and felt yourself wilting in the heat of disappointment, disease, or distress? When those seasons come, choose to trust God—his faithfulness is true. Draw from the well of God's living Word. A time of refreshing rain will come. God will not abandon you.

DAY 341

2 Timothy 2:11–13

*The saying is trustworthy, for: If we have died with him,
we will also live with him; if we endure, we will also reign
with him; if we deny him, he also will deny us; if we are
faithless, he remains faithful—for he cannot deny himself.*

List ways God has been faithful to you, even when you haven't
always been faithful to him. What does your list say about God?

The right faith relies on God's faithfulness. God cannot reject
his children. He cannot prevent the soul he has attracted
from receiving good. Even if we are unfaithful, he remains
faithful. Forget the estimations of the power of your faith or
of the searching of its roots or of analyzing its components.
Start by keeping in mind the impossibility for God to give up
his own self. This is how the true faith will be born in you.
Looking toward God's faithfulness, your faith will become so
strong, that it will move mountains.

Richard Wurmbrand

WHOM SHALL I FEAR?

DAY 342

Ezekiel 34:22, 24

"I will rescue my flock; they shall no longer be a prey.
And I will judge between sheep and sheep....And I, the
Lord, will be their God, and my servant David shall be
prince among them. I am the Lord; I have spoken."

A man in Laos turned to faith in Jesus Christ. His family and community became incensed over his decision to follow Jesus. They confronted him and angrily beat him until he lost consciousness. A friend brought the man to his home to recuperate. Since this incident, they beat him ten additional times. He testified, "The trials I have gone through have served to strengthen my faith, and I see God's faithfulness in delivering me. I thank God I have been able to bring thirty people to the saving knowledge of Jesus."

Your faithfulness may be interrupted by fear, but God's steadfast loyalty to you never ends. Take time today to thank God for his loyalty to you.

DAY 343

Joel 2:21–22

"Fear not, O land; be glad and rejoice, for the LORD has done great things! Fear not, you beasts of the field, for the pastures of the wilderness are green; the tree bears its fruit; the fig tree and vine give their full yield."

At first, pallets of Bibles sitting in a warehouse in the Middle East were a hopeful sign. But it looked increasingly unlikely they would ever reach the hands of the Iranian believers for whom they were intended. Suddenly, on Christmas Eve, God opened a door, and front-line workers were able to smuggle a batch of Bibles into Iran where it is illegal to own, print, import, or distribute Bibles. The Bible distribution continued into the next year. Thousands more crossed into Iran and were distributed to a vibrant house church network. The house churches then gave the Bibles to Christians who didn't own a copy.

Fear not—God has done great things in days past and will continue to do great things again. Proclaim this truth again and again.

DAY 344

Habakkuk 3:17–18

Though the fig tree should not blossom, nor fruit be on the vines, the produce of the olive fail and the fields yield no food, the flock be cut off from the fold and there be no herd in the stalls, yet I will rejoice in the LORD; I will take joy in the God of my salvation.

Lord, my persecuted Christian brothers and sisters count the cost for their obedience. They suffer greatly at the hands of those who oppose them because of their commitment to you. Hold them close as they face hunger and danger. Let them know they're not alone and that you will faithfully be with them. Give them the strength to choose joy amid suffering. Give them your peace that passes all understanding. Amen.

DAY 345

Matthew 6:25–29, 33–34

"Therefore I tell you, do not be anxious about your life, what you will eat or what you will drink, nor about your body, what you will put on. Is not life more than food, and the body more than clothing? Look at the birds of the air: they neither sow nor reap nor gather into barns, and yet your heavenly Father feeds them. Are you not of more value than they? And which of you by being anxious can add a single hour to his span of life? And why are you anxious about clothing? Consider the lilies of the field, how they grow: they neither toil nor spin, yet I tell you, even Solomon in all his glory was not arrayed like one of these. But seek first the kingdom of God and his righteousness, and all these things will be added to you. Therefore do not be anxious about tomorrow, for tomorrow will be anxious for itself. Sufficient for the day is its own trouble."

Today, despite your circumstances, thank the Lord for his continual faithfulness to you.

DAY 346

John 14:1–4

"Let not your hearts be troubled. Believe in God;
believe also in me. In my Father's house are many
rooms. If it were not so, would I have told you that
I go to prepare a place for you? And if I go and pre-
pare a place for you, I will come again and will take
you to myself, that where I am you may be also."

Growing up as a Muslim in Kenya, Abdiwelli wrestled with doubts about the afterlife. Islam's works-based view of salvation left Abdiwelli feeling empty and insecure. But when he read Jesus' words in John 14, Abdiwelli found the eternal security he had long desired. Abdiwelli placed his trust in Christ. Like Abdiwelli, you can find hope in the words of Jesus Christ. One day, Jesus will return and take you with him to the place he has prepared for you. There is nothing to fear.

DAY 347

1 Corinthians 10:13

No temptation has overtaken you that is not common to man. God is faithful, and he will not let you be tempted beyond your ability, but with the temptation he will also provide the way of escape, that you may be able to endure it.

During his 445-day imprisonment in the Sudan, Petr Jasek scratched this verse onto the walls of his prison cell as a reminder of God's faithful provision when he was tempted to despair. What are you tempted by today? Like an illuminated exit sign showing the way out when danger arises, God provides an exit from temptation too. Where is the exit he has provided for you? Are you willing to take it?

DAY 348

Deuteronomy 7:9

*"Know therefore that the L*ORD *your God is God,
the faithful God who keeps covenant and steadfast love with those who love him and keep his
commandments, to a thousand generations."*

In parts of Africa, Muslims try to lure children in majority-Christian villages away from the Christian faith by offering them free Islamic education which includes room and board. Teenagers have even been radicalized in exchange for material benefits. After children's Bibles were distributed in an African country where Islam was spreading quickly, a front-line worker shared: "I am sure by the grace of God . . . we will have a strong future for the church, as the young generation will be equipped with the Word of God, and hence will not be deceived by any false doctrine or religion. They will be able to know what they believe and why they believe in it, which is the Lord Jesus."

How is God calling you to help disciple the next generation?

DAY 349

2 Corinthians 4:13–18

Since we have the same spirit of faith according to what has been written, "I believed, and so I spoke," we also believe, . . . knowing that he who raised the Lord Jesus will raise us also with Jesus and bring us with you into his presence. For it is all for your sake, so that as grace extends to more and more people it may increase thanksgiving, to the glory of God. So we do not lose heart. Though our outer self is wasting away, our inner self is being renewed day by day. For this light momentary affliction is preparing for us an eternal weight of glory beyond all comparison, as we look not to the things that are seen but to the things that are unseen. For the things that are seen are transient, but the things that are unseen are eternal.

Our persecuted brothers and sisters can have confidence in the hope of resurrection. Through Christ's faithfulness on the cross, they look forward, with hope, to be reunited with him. And we share that hope with them.

DAY 350

Lamentations 3:22–25

*The steadfast love of the L*ORD *never ceases; his mercies never come to an end; they are new every morning; great is your faithfulness. "The L*ORD *is my portion," says my soul, "therefore I will hope in him." The L*ORD *is good to those who wait for him, to the soul who seeks him.*

Lord, thank you, thank you, thank you for your steadfast love, for mercies that never end, and for faithfulness that washes away my fears. Open my eyes to see how you are going before me, how you are working in and through me. In you alone, Lord, I find hope. In you, I find life. Today, I pray that you would provide me with an opportunity to share about your faithfulness with someone who needs to hear it. Amen.

DAY 351

Philippians 1:6

And I am sure of this, that he who began a good work in you will bring it to completion at the day of Jesus Christ.

Name three things you're certain of in this life. None of those things are more certain than God's promise to bring his good work to completion in you. He's faithful to continue working in and through you, so don't let fear distract you. Nothing you encounter today will come as a surprise to God.

DAY 352

Colossians 3:1-4

*If then you have been raised with Christ, seek the things
that are above, where Christ is, seated at the right hand
of God. Set your minds on things that are above, not on
things that are on earth. For you have died, and your life
is hidden with Christ in God. When Christ who is your
life appears, then you also will appear with him in glory.*

Many of our persecuted Christian brothers and sisters daily practice the discipline of setting their minds on things above. At
this very moment, they choose to look beyond prison walls to focus on
their Lord in heaven. They choose forgiveness rather than revenge, love
rather than hate, trust instead of fear. With Jesus Christ's help, can you
look beyond your circumstances and do the same?

The Richness of God in Our Hearts

By Sabina Wurmbrand

In 2 Kings 4:7, we read about a widow who cries to Elisha for help because she is unable to repay a debt. She knows that if the debt is not repaid, the creditor will take her two sons as slaves. After the woman tells Elisha that she has nothing but a single jar of oil in the entire house, he provides her with a miraculous example of her true riches in God.

This passage never meant more to me than when I was being held in Communist prisons.

Romania is a country of 20 million people, and every tenth man or woman was imprisoned or forced into slave labor. When the men were arrested, the women took their place. The Communists were shocked to see Christian women working in this way, and when they saw that we really meant it, they arrested thousands of us.

When we were in prison, we were very poor. We were hungry, we were beaten, and we were very dirty. I remember a Christian lady who was humiliated by a prison official after being taken out of her underground prison cell. He took out a mirror and gave it to our sister. "Look how beautiful you are," he said in mockery. "Why are you so foolish? Why do you speak about God?"

When she saw herself in the mirror, she could barely recognize herself. The Communist officer enjoyed her misery. "Just sign this statement and you will be home with your children," he said. Mentioning her children was like a stab to the heart. She immediately began to cry and became unsure of how to answer.

A few seconds later, however, the Holy Spirit gave her the right answer. "Mr. Officer," she said, "I know my children are in your hands, but I still cannot deny my Lord. For it is written in our Bible that one day every knee will bow before our Lord and Master. Even you, Mr. Officer, will have to bend your knees before Him."

The officer went into a rage. He beat the woman and sent her back to the prison cell.

Many years later, we learned how God had richly blessed her witness.

> "NOBODY COULD TAKE WHAT WAS IN OUR HEARTS."

After a time of crisis, when the officer's wife had run away with one of his colleagues, this officer who had beaten the Christians, bent his knees humbly before Jesus as his Lord and Savior. God had blessed the Christian woman's witness, using it to draw the hater of God to himself.

While we were very poor, our greatest need was the work of God. In this great poverty, we discovered how rich we were, just as the widow discovered her own riches—in the form of an endless oil supply—by crying out to God's prophet Elisha.

Everything had been taken from us, but nobody could take what was in our hearts. We saw how one word from the Bible brought new light, new hope. Lives were saved by this richness.

Jesus hears the cry of your heart. Today he would tell you, "I know what you need." Today would you look in your heart? What do you have? We never understood this question so well as when we understood it in prison.

Christians are locked up in asylums with madmen simply because they love Jesus. They are gagged and placed in straight jackets. I ask you to hear their cry.

In hearing their cry and seeing their tears, I ask you to join them in their tears.

Soon our Lord will return, and He will wipe away our many tears. I know you have your problems, and Jesus knows them, too. But the tears you shed for others will be the most valuable, like diamonds.

Let the cry of suffering Christians be heard in your heart, in your home, in your churches. They need your prayers. They need your help. They need your tears of compassion. Join hands with them.

Sometimes as we sat in the dark prison cell with tears on our faces, our hearts were near fainting. There was no help from anywhere. Then Jesus himself would lift the veil for a second. We saw heavenly glory. We heard heavenly music. New strength and new joy filled our hearts.

Christians came out of the depths of suffering stronger and richer because Jesus himself had enriched us, fought for us, and made us to understand what it means.

Wonderful is his name.

DAY 353

Psalm 71:5–6

For you, O Lord, are my hope, my trust, O LORD,
from my youth. Upon you I have leaned from
before my birth; you are he who took me from my
mother's womb. My praise is continually of you.

Draw a brief timeline of your life below. Mark places along the way that God has been faithful to you. Thank him for his faithfulness in the past. Then thank him for his faithfulness despite what you will face in the future.

DAY 354

1 Thessalonians 5:23–24

*Now may the God of peace himself sanctify you com-
pletely, and may your whole spirit and soul and body be
kept blameless at the coming of our Lord Jesus Christ.
He who calls you is faithful; he will surely do it.*

P romises made, promises kept—that's the faithfulness of God. He's
promised to never forget or forsake you. How does that promise
change how you handle the hard things in your life? Use the space below to write down your response.

DAY 355

Proverbs 3:21–26

*My son, do not lose sight of these—keep sound wisdom
and discretion, and they will be life for your soul and
adornment for your neck. Then you will walk on your way
securely, and your foot will not stumble. If you lie down,
you will not be afraid; when you lie down, your sleep will
be sweet. Do not be afraid of sudden terror or of the ruin
of the wicked, when it comes, for the Lord will be your
confidence and will keep your foot from being caught.*

How often do you "lose sight" of a truth you know? How can you correct it and refocus on the truth of God's faithfulness? God is faithful, and you shall not fear. Perhaps there is someone in your world who has lost sight of God's faithfulness. Ask God to show you who that is, and reach out to that person with a reminder: God is with them.

DAY 356

2 Timothy 1:8–12

*Therefore do not be ashamed of the testimony about
our Lord, nor of me his prisoner, but share in suffering
for the gospel by the power of God, who saved us and
called us to a holy calling, not because of our works but
because of his own purpose and grace, which he gave us
in Christ Jesus before the ages began, and which now
has been manifested through the appearing of our Savior
Christ Jesus, who abolished death and brought life and
immortality to light through the gospel, for which I was
appointed a preacher and apostle and teacher, which is
why I suffer as I do. But I am not ashamed, for I know
whom I have believed, and I am convinced that he is able
to guard until that day what has been entrusted to me.*

Today is the day to be bold. Through word and deed, boldly share
the gospel with someone.

DAY 357

Psalm 42:8-11

*By day the L*ORD *commands his steadfast love, and at night
his song is with me, a prayer to the God of my life. I say
to God, my rock: "Why have you forgotten me? Why do
I go mourning because of the oppression of the enemy?"
As with a deadly wound in my bones, my adversaries
taunt me, while they say to me all the day long, "Where
is your God?" Why are you cast down, O my soul, and
why are you in turmoil within me? Hope in God; for
I shall again praise him, my salvation and my God.*

After radical Hindus in India killed Bindi's husband because of his Christian faith, she did not lose hope in God. Instead, she said she has learned more about God's faithfulness and purposes since her husband's death. "God has provided what I need," she said. "God is teaching me to remain strong so I can make other women strong." How does Bindi's testimony encourage you to hope in God and to trust his faithfulness?

DAY 358

Titus 1:1–3

Paul, a servant of God and an apostle of Jesus Christ,
for the sake of the faith of God's elect and their knowl-
edge of the truth, which accords with godliness, in hope
of eternal life, which God, who never lies, promised
before the ages began and at the proper time manifested
in his word through the preaching with which I have
been entrusted by the command of God our Savior.

G od never lies. He is faithful always. He is truthful always. What
does this mean to you today? What truths from God do you
struggle to accept?

> God is testing our faith, our courage, and our patience at this
> time. But God will never abandon Christians. It is during the
> high seas that the good sailor stands out, and it is during the
> time of tribulations that the good Christian does the same.
>
> Chrysostomos in his final sermon
> before he was martyred (Turkey, 1922)

WHOM SHALL I FEAR?

DAY 359

Hebrews 10:23

Let us hold fast the confession of our hope without
wavering, for he who promised is faithful.

I f you are scourged or beheaded as a criminal, do you believe you
will still ascend to heaven?" asked Rusticus, the Roman city official.
"I believe that if I endure these things I shall have what Jesus promised
me," Justin said. "For I know his gift of life stays with all who remain in
him, even until the end of the world." Justin was martyred for his faith.

One mark of biblical discipleship is an untroubled heart, focused
on God's promise of an eternal reward. No threat or anxiety can move
those whose heart is fixed on such promises.

Lord, you never falter. You never fail. Your faithfulness to your
promises is absolute, unyielding, and the bedrock on which I can build
my life. Give me a faith in you that's just as true and a trust that is un-
wavering. I cling to you, Lord. You are my refuge and fortress. Amen.

DAY 360

Isaiah 50:7

But the Lord GOD helps me; therefore, I have not
been disgraced; therefore, I have set my face like a
flint, and I know that I shall not be put to shame.

God is faithfully with you—always. How does knowing that shift
your view of those things that frighten you? List them below and
give them to the Lord.

May we live a life with a shining face, with a smile, with a
song, as [those] who have an eternity of paradise before us!
Richard Wurmbrand

DAY 361

Psalm 146:5–8

Blessed is he whose help is the God of Jacob, whose hope is in the LORD his God, who made heaven and earth, the sea, and all that is in them, who keeps faith forever; who executes justice for the oppressed, who gives food to the hungry. The LORD sets the prisoners free; the LORD opens the eyes of the blind. The LORD lifts up those who are bowed down; the LORD loves the righteous.

Lord, sometimes it seems as though I'm a prisoner of my fears. I can't break free. Draw my eyes away from those things that frighten me and set them on you. Set my heart on the hope I have in you. You are mightier than anything that threatens me, Lord. I lay my fears before you and ask you to heal me. Amen.

DAY 362

1 Peter 1:6–9

In this you rejoice, though now for a little while, if necessary, you have been grieved by various trials, so that the tested genuineness of your faith—more precious than gold that perishes though it is tested by fire—may be found to result in praise and glory and honor at the revelation of Jesus Christ. Though you have not seen him, you love him. Though you do not now see him, you believe in him and rejoice with joy that is inexpressible and filled with glory, obtaining the outcome of your faith, the salvation of your souls.

Those words—for a little while—comfort our persecuted Christian brothers and sisters. Yes, there's suffering now, but it won't last forever. Yes, proclaiming Christ now brings torture and imprisonment, but a day is coming when all will proclaim Christ. Embrace those four small words: for a little while.

DAY 363

1 John 5:13

I write these things to you who believe in the name of the
Son of God, that you may know that you have eternal life.

God's promise of eternal life can free you to obey him with boldness. Why? While your earthly life is something you cannot keep, you can be confident that you have eternal life through faith in Jesus Christ. So cling to what is eternal—Jesus. Ask God to help you set aside fear and choose to trust him instead.

DAY 364

Psalm 36:5–8

*Your steadfast love, O L*ORD*, extends to the heavens,*
your faithfulness to the clouds. Your righteousness is
like the mountains of God; your judgments are like
*the great deep; man and beast you save, O L*ORD*. How*
precious is your steadfast love, O God! The children
of mankind take refuge in the shadow of your wings.
They feast on the abundance of your house, and you
give them drink from the river of your delights.

This poetic passage is a reminder of God's great faithfulness and of his love that is beyond measure. After reading the Psalm, how does it change your perspective of the fears you are facing?

DAY 365

Psalm 26:3

For your steadfast love is before my eyes,
and I walk in your faithfulness.

List the ways you see God's steadfast love poured out to you. Thank him for his faithfulness—and walk in that love.

DAY 366

Revelation 21:3-4

And I heard a loud voice from the throne saying, "Behold, the dwelling place of God is with man. He will dwell with them, and they will be his people, and God himself will be with them as their God. He will wipe away every tear from their eyes, and death shall be no more, neither shall there be mourning, nor crying, nor pain anymore, for the former things have passed away."

A time is coming when hospitals and funeral homes will be no more. Those who dwell with God will do so in eternal comfort and gratitude. This certainty gives those facing pain and persecution for their faithful witness an eternal perspective and a shining hope. Our God is good!

Conclusion

What now? Overcoming fear is a daily challenge. Satan, though a defeated foe (Matthew 25:41), doesn't give up easily. He will continue to lie (John 8:44), seeking only to steal, kill, and destroy (John 10:10). Satan's goal is to keep God's people from obeying the Great Commission.

But that foe can be defeated as we anchor our lives in the Word of God (Revelation 12:11)!

As you continue in this pursuit, consider several ongoing disciplines:

- Read, memorize, and internalize God's Word. The truth of God's Word will overcome fear and every negative emotion we face.

- Walk in obedience to what you know. Christ has given us every instruction we need to live obediently (Matthew 28:18–20), and he has given us all the power we need to do so (Acts 1:8). Christians often think they need more knowledge, but that is a misconception. As biblical disciples walk in obedience to the knowledge they already possess, their maturity grows exponentially.

- Continue to be encouraged and inspired by the stories of our persecuted Christian family members through VOM's free monthly magazine. Our brothers and sisters living on the world's most difficult and dangerous mission fields exemplify the power of obedience to Christ over fear. Visit vom.org/subscribe, or call 800-747-0085 to request your free subscription.

May God richly bless you as you walk in confident obedience, conquering fear along the way!

About The Voice of the Martyrs

The Voice of the Martyrs (VOM) is a nonprofit, interdenominational Christian organization dedicated to serving persecuted Christians on the world's most difficult and dangerous mission fields and bringing other members of the body of Christ into fellowship with them. VOM was founded in 1967 by Pastor Richard Wurmbrand and his wife, Sabina. Richard was imprisoned fourteen years in Communist Romania for his faith in Christ, and Sabina was imprisoned for three years. They were ransomed out of Romania in 1965 and soon established a global network of missions dedicated to assisting persecuted Christians.

To be inspired by the courageous faith of our persecuted brothers and sisters in Christ who are advancing the gospel in hostile areas and restricted nations, request a free subscription to VOM's award-winning monthly magazine. Visit us at vom.org, or call 800-747-0085.

To learn more about VOM's work, please contact us:

United States	vom.org
Australia	vom.com.au
Belgium	hvk-aem.be
Brazil	maisnomundo.org
Canada	vomcanada.com
Czech Republic	hlas-mucedniku.cz
Finland	marttyyrienaani.fi
Germany	verfolgte-christen.org
The Netherlands	sdok.nl

New Zealand	vom.org.nz
Poland	gpch.pl
Portugal	vozdosmartires.com
Singapore	gosheninternational.org
South Africa	persecutionsa.org
South Korea	vomkorea.kr
United Kingdom	releaseinternational.org

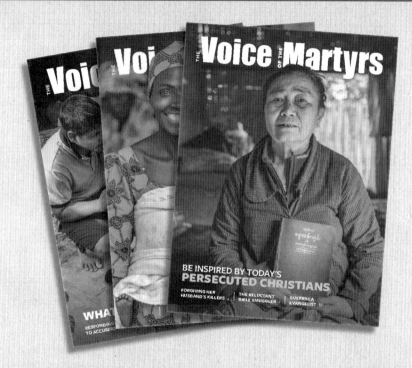

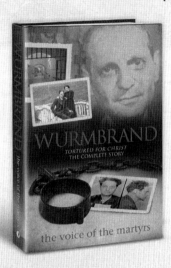

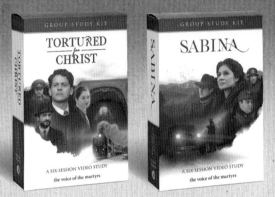

GET THE FULL STORY

Richard and Sabina Wurmbrand, founders of The Voice of the Martyrs, boldly witnessed for Christ amid Nazi and Communist oppression in Romania. Their full story can now be experienced for free in two award-winning feature films.

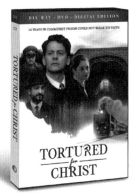

Tortured for Christ — The Movie

This is a cinematic retelling of VOM founder Richard Wurmbrand's testimony, as written in his international bestseller *Tortured for Christ*. Filmed entirely in Romania, including in the very prison where Richard endured torture and solitary confinement, this powerful film will challenge every viewer to consider what it means to sacrifice for following Jesus Christ.

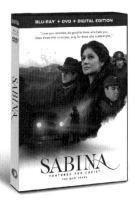

Sabina: Tortured for Christ, the Nazi Years

See how God's love transformed an ambitious, atheistic hedonist into one of the greatest Christian women of the 20th century. After Nazis killed her entire family, Sabina Wurmbrand risked her own life to share the love and truth of Christ with them. Experience the amazing true story that has inspired millions around the world.

To view both movies on-demand for free, visit
vom.org/WurmbrandMovies.

INSPIRE KIDS AND TEENS

WITNESSES TRILOGY BOXED SET

These three animated films take you from Christ's birth through the birth of the early church. Inspire children and young adults with the retelling of Christ's life and sacrificial death, and watch as His followers take His message to the ends of the earth.

THE TORCHLIGHTERS ULTIMATE ACTIVITY BOOK AND DVD SET

The Voice of the Martyrs presents a 144-page, full-color activity book to complement the award-winning Torchlighters DVD series.

VOM GRAPHIC NOVEL

This full-color, graphic novel anthology covers the earliest period of church history — from A.D. 34 to A.D. 203 — including the time of the apostles and early church martyrs.

COURAGEOUS SERIES

Inspire your children with the true stories of biblical heroes and saints. VOM's Courageous Series books highlight the lives of faithful Christians from history, showing how they boldly proclaimed Christ in the face of persecution. Includes the stories of Stephen, Thomas, the Apostle Paul, Nicholas, Patrick and Valentine.

FREE RESOURCES

CHOOSE ONE OF THESE RESOURCES FOR FREE AT **VOM.ORG/KIDS-FREE**